I0883251

UNDERSTANDING JONATHAN COE

UNDERSTANDING CONTEMPORARY BRITISH LITERATURE

Matthew J. Bruccoli, Founding Editor

Understanding Kingsley Amis
Merritt Moseley

Understanding Martin Amis
James Diedrick

Understanding Beryl Bainbridge
Brett Josef Grubisic

Understanding Julian Barnes
Merritt Moseley

Understanding Alan Bennett
Peter Wolfe

Understanding Anita Brookner
Cheryl Alexander Malcolm

Understanding Jonathan Coe
Merritt Moseley

Understanding John Fowles
Thomas C. Foster

Understanding Michael Frayn
Merrit Moseley

Understanding Graham Greene
R. H. Miller

Understanding Kazuo Ishiguro
Brian W. Shaffer

Understanding John le Carré
John L. Cobbs

Understanding Doris Lessing
Jean Pickering

Understanding Ian McEwan
David Malcolm

Understanding Iris Murdoch
Cheryl K. Bove

Understanding Tim Parks
Gillian Fenwick

Understanding Harold Pinter
Ronald Knowles

Understanding Anthony Powell
Nicholas Birns

Understanding Will Self
M. Hunter Hayes

Understanding Alan Sillitoe
Gillian Mary Hanson

Understanding Graham Swift
David Malcolm

Understanding Arnold Wesker
Robert Wilcher

Understanding Paul West
David W. Madden

UNDERSTANDING

Jonathan Coe

Merritt Moseley

THE UNIVERSITY OF SOUTH CAROLINA PRESS

© 2016 University of South Carolina

Published by the University of South Carolina Press
Columbia, South Carolina 29208

www.sc.edu/uscpress

Manufactured in the United States of America

24 23 22 21 20 19 18 17 16
10 9 8 7 6 5 4 3 2 1

Library of Congress Cataloging-in-Publication Data
can be found at http://catalog.loc.gov/.

ISBN: 978-1-61117-650-6 (cloth)
ISBN: 978-1-61117-651-3 (ebook)

This book was printed on recycled paper with
30 percent postconsumer waste content.

To Madeline, once again, with my love

CONTENTS

SERIES EDITOR'S PREFACE

The volumes of Understanding Contemporary British Literature have been planned as guides or companions for students as well as good nonacademic readers. The editor and publisher perceive a need for these volumes because much of the influential contemporary literature makes special demands. Uninitiated readers encounter difficulty in approaching works that depart from the traditional forms and techniques of prose and poetry. Literature relies on conventions, but the conventions keep evolving; new writers form their own conventions—which in time may become familiar. Put simply, UCBL provides instruction in how to read certain contemporary writers—identifying and explicating their material, themes, use of language, point of view, structures, symbolism, and responses to experience.

The word *understanding* in the titles was deliberately chosen. Many willing readers lack an adequate understanding of how contemporary literature works; that is, what the author is attempting to express and the means by which it is conveyed. Although the criticism and analysis in the series have been aimed at a level of general accessibility, these introductory volumes are meant to be applied in conjunction with the works they cover. They do not provide a substitute for the works and authors they introduce, but rather prepare the reader for more profitable literary experiences.

M.J.B.

PREFACE

The book that follows is designed to introduce new readers to the work of Jonathan Coe and to help (and encourage) those who have already become his readers. It is designed as a guide accessible to any interested and intelligent reader, without requiring extensive knowledge of contemporary literary theory, the British literary scene, or other specialized domains.

The title, *Understanding Jonathan Coe,* is not meant to insist that Coe's writing is abstruse or forbidding or that readers are helpless to understand it without outside assistance. Instead it implies that a deeper study, assisted by discussion of some important features, can produce more understanding, and—as an additional desirable outcome—enhanced appreciation and enjoyment of the novels. Jonathan Coe is a writer who wishes his readers to read his books with pleasure, rather than as an ordeal or obligation. May this book help them to increase that pleasure.

As always, I am indebted to the helpful and cheerful librarians of my academic library at the University of North Carolina at Asheville; to my colleagues for their encouragement, their efforts sustaining the necessary work of our department, and their examples of serious and penetrating reading of texts; and to Jonathan Coe, for friendly approachability. I appreciate them all.

Finally, I thank my family—my daughters, their partners, and my grandchildren—for their affection and the joy they bring to my life and most of all, for all that I owe her, my wife, Madeline.

ONE

Understanding Jonathan Coe

Jonathan Coe, the author of ten novels, is recognized as one of the most important and most consistently rewarding novelists of his generation (he was born in 1961). His contemporary Nick Hornby calls him "probably the best English novelist of his generation."[1] His output includes vertiginously experimental fictions, broad-canvassed depictions of British society, political satire, and careful delineations of lonely or frustrated individuals. Hornby's tribute comes in a review of Coe's biography of B. S. Johnson, as Coe is also accomplished as a biographer, reviewer, and commentator.

Florence Noiville has summed up the Coe characteristics as a "subtle interaction between the public and the private, of constant comings and goings between the serious and the unusual, and of course, humour, but never too much of it: This is Coe's method."[2] Noiville comments mostly on his themes; in an essay tellingly called "The Best Writer You've Never Heard Of"—in other words, a writer you will not have heard of if you are an American—Steven Zeitchik writes that "Coe's attention to wit and character, and his treatment of the novel as a puzzle with many movable narrative parts, ensures that this books are, uncommonly, both artful and highly enjoyable."[3]

The novelist with a postgraduate literary education, like the novel-writing don, is less common in Britain than in the United States, and, although Jonathan Coe received a Ph.D. from Warwick University, he clearly did not plan on a university career. He had been a part-time writer since adolescence and even earlier; he very quickly became a full-time writer. The legacy of his academic study may appear most importantly in the willingness of his novels to flaunt their own fictionality, like the fiction of Henry Fielding and Samuel Beckett, subjects of his Ph.D. and M.A. theses. He began writing fiction at the age of eight, sent his first full-length novel to a publisher when he was fifteen, and wrote fiction at Cambridge, and it is understandable that full-time writing (which continues to include reviewing, especially in the *London Review of Books,* as well as the authorship of three nonfiction books) has been his adult career.

After failing to emerge from critical obscurity with his first three novels, Coe bloomed into a widely acclaimed and highly visible novelist of the first rank with his fourth book, *What a Carve Up!* Since that time, his books have sold widely and have been well received by reviewers. Among the tributes to him is the assertion by Robert Hanks, in 2004, that "with the withering of Martin Amis's talent, Jonathan Coe is now the funniest serious novelist practicing in this country."[4] The American critic Richard Eder wrote in 1998 that "Jonathan Coe is the late Kingsley Amis' most talented successor in employing the refreshment of dismay to denounce the state of Britain and beyond. Appropriately contrarian, he stands in the opposite corner from his predecessor."[5] That is, he denounces from the left as Amis did from the right.

Coe is not particularly vocal in talking about his own work, but some of his literary aims may be deduced from a criticism he made of the literary novel in the 1990s: "the majority of literary novels being published here at the moment, while full of intelligent ideas and in general very accomplished stylistically, are none the less weak on plot, weak on character and shy of formal innovation: somehow, it would seem, we have evolved a brand of novel that contrives at once to be both middlebrow and deeply, irredeemably unpopular. As a result, the literary novel is now at the very margins of cultural life in England."[6] Although he does not say so in this commentary, his own ten novels go some way toward disproving his generally gloomy assessment, in part because they are strongly plotted and bold in formal innovation.

Jonathan Coe was born on August 19, 1961, in Lickey, a suburb of Birmingham. It is a striking feature of his work that he is so loyal to the setting of his birth and early life. He has called himself a "provincial," and most of his novels feature suburban Birmingham and the Lickey Hills.[7] The best example is found in *The Rotters' Club,* where Benjamin Trotter, something of a traditional, family-oriented boy, thinks about "the Lickey Hills, where his grandparents lived, and where he was heading that same afternoon. It wasn't just the slow inclines and occasional muted, autumnal glades of this semi-pastoral backwater that made him think of the Shire [that is, in Tolkien]; the inhabitants themselves were hobbit-like, in their breezy indifference towards the wider world, their unchallenged certainty that they were living the best of all possible lives in the best of all possible locations."[8]

Alongside his birth in the Midlands, much about his early life is rather ordinary. His middle-class family—his father was a physicist, his mother a teacher of music and physical education—belonged to the Church of England and inhabited a three-bedroom house in what's called a "leafy suburb." His parents were Tory voters, and he has said he would have been, too, at that time. His early reading tended toward P. G. Wodehouse and Arthur Conan Doyle: his interests came more from his grandfather than from his parents, who were not readers, particularly. He was also devoted to rock and roll, television (which he has called his "main source of narrative" in the 1970s), and movies, to which his novels often make reference.[9] Without apology he displays great loyalty toward such popular films as *What a Carve Up!* and *The Private Life of Sherlock Holmes.* For a time he was the film critic for the *New Statesman,* and he writes about film criticism in his fiction, often with some irony. He attended King Edward's School, an independent day school for boys founded in the sixteenth century; from there he matriculated at Trinity College, Cambridge, and followed his bachelor's degree with an M.A. and a Ph.D., earned at Warwick University. Obviously an able academic, he was not drawn to the teaching profession and while pursuing his degree was continuing to write fiction. He acknowledges four still unpublished novels written before he had any success.

That success, although initially very modest, came with the writing of *The Accidental Woman* (1987). He has explained that it grew out of a violent dislike for his male protagonists. He was then living in Coventry and submitted his books, unsuccessfully, for some time before the publishers Duckworth took *The Accidental Woman.* This novel probably best exemplifies the account of his early fiction given by Philip Tew as "combining a reflexive, self-aware experimentation with a blend of caricature and satirical, ironic distance" (47). He was paid £200 for what he has called the literary nonevent of the '80s.

He then moved to London, where he was trying to launch a career in rock music. He took a job proofreading legal documents in a solicitors' office and there began to share proofreading tasks with a young woman named Janine Maria McKeown, whom he later married. They have two daughters, Matilda and Madeline.

His next novel, *A Touch of Love,* made no more of a sensation in the publishing world than *The Accidental Woman,* although the publisher did pay him twice as much for it. It is about a troubled graduate student, living in Coventry (the location of the University of Warwick, where Coe earned his Ph.D.). In his third published book, *The Dwarves of Death,* his own musical ambitions and life as a poor young graduate living in London are artfully incorporated into a lurid tale including murder by dwarves.

In 1994 his career took an important turn. He has explained the origins of his changed direction: "With *What a Carve Up!* I knew I wanted to do a big political novel, alongside this personal story about my childhood. The way into it I found was to write about the films I'd been obsessed with when I was a child, the one I recalled most strongly being that film, and when I made that choice to use, the political idea immediately came to be at the same time, because I thought What a Carve Up is the title I want for a novel about the Thatcher years."[10] This longer and much more ambitious novel, which required research undemanded by his earlier books, took several years to write, and to support himself and his family during the writing he undertook two biographies of American film stars: *Humphrey Bogart: Take It and Like It* (1991) and *Jimmy Stewart: A Wonderful Life* (1994).

Clearly his own adult political stance as woven into *What a Carve Up!* had shifted away from the middle-England Toryism of his family; Coe has been one of the most openly political novelists of his generation, writing from a sometimes fiery left-liberal position about the ruthlessness and greed that, although obviously not invented by Margaret Thatcher or in the 1980s, he suggests were elevated into a national policy and granted the status of desirable values at that time. As time went on he was to be bitterly disappointed by the Labor succession to the Thatcher/Major years, believing that it was sufficiently oppositional and that Blairite Labor had abandoned the historic socialist principles of the party. Beyond the domestic politics of democratic and economic egalitarianism, he has also staked out strong positions in his fiction for equal treatment of women and—even more insistently—in opposition to military adventurism, especially British collusion with U.S. adventurism in the Middle East.

What a Carve Up! attracted favorable reaction both by its inventively political narrative and by its innovative form. The title comes from and pays tribute to a British horror/comedy film of the same name. Michael Owen, the protagonist, has been obsessed with the film since watching it as a boy, the plot makes use of elements of the film, and the title also suggests the carving-up of the nation and its culture by the ruthless and privileged rich. The book also refers to the novel from which the film was made (*The Ghoul* by Frank King). It includes broad satire, pastiche, and self-referential narrative.

Sally Vincent points to *What a Carve Up!* as "his fourth published novel, but the first to be panoramic in ambition and noticeable in impact" such that "literary critics uniformly raved about its brilliance, its sociological and political acuity and its general, all-round hilarity."[11] She exaggerates when she goes on to say that Coe was crowned the "prince of postmodernism," but that feature of his fiction, actually more visible in some of his early novels but of course visible only to their small number of readers, is one of the materials that form the entirely original mixture of his novels.

It was a success not only in the United Kingdom but abroad; translated into sixteen languages, it won the Prix du Meilleur Livre Étranger, an award given annually since 1948 to a foreign language book by a group of literary directors in France. It is a curious feature of Coe's career that his books may well be more admired in France than in England; he also has enjoyed great critical and popular success in Italy and Greece. Paul Laity claims that his "biggest audience by far is on the continent," and Coe offers this explanation: the French "feel rather starved of novels which feature strong narratives, humour, and engagement with contemporary social issues."[12] In the United States it was published in 1995 as *The Winshaw Legacy;* this is the title of the history that, in the novel, the narrator, Michael Owen, is writing; the Winshaws are the horrible family at the heart of the novel, and presumably American audiences would not recognize the British film alluded to in Coe's title, because, on its American release, it was retitled *No Place Like Homicide.*

His next novel, 1997's *The House of Sleep,* although not as panoramic as its predecessor, shared with it a political edge, particularly in its focus on a conscience-free scientist and privatized health care; formal inventiveness, with dual temporal schemes united by a house and its past and present inhabitants, a dazzling variety of documents including a film review, personal letters, film treatments, a poem, a transcription of a patient talking in her sleep, and a hilariously botched profile of a film director; and a concern with popular culture alongside "high" culture (*The House of Sleep,* which plays an important role in the plot, is the name of a real novel by Frank King, author of the source novel for *What a Carve Up!*). Underneath the humor and the textual fun is an awareness of the sadness of many lives. Coe is very reluctant to write autobiographically, although he has acknowledged some history of sleepwalking, which may have stimulated his use of a sleep clinic in this novel. *The House of Sleep* won the Prix Médicis Étranger; the Prix Médicis is an award given since 1958 to an underappreciated author, and the Prix Médicis Etranger is a version of the prize for books translated into French.

In his next novel Coe took a surprising turn toward a combination of coming-of-age narrative and the condition-of-England novel. The period chosen was the 1970s, the era of his own youth, and the setting—a suburban milieu in the Lickey area of the West Midlands, featuring teenagers who attend a school (or two schools, one for each sex) like his own King Edward's School, suggests a movement in the direction of autobiography, although the plot has little to do with the author's own life. Coe does still think of himself as a Birmingham writer, even "a provincial writer."[13] *The Rotters' Club* is about a loosely affiliated group of young people, more centrally the Trotter family and particularly Ben Trotter. They live through political crises—race, labor unrest, IRA incendiarism—as well as the usual adolescent problems with love, friendship, and families.

Although *The Rotters' Club* is not the sort of book that earns an author the title of the prince of postmodernism, it is risk-taking in several ways. It ends with a fifteen-thousand-word-long sentence that, according to Sally Vincent, "as a triumph of form over content . . . has to be seen to be believed" (36). But the more important accomplishment in this novel is its inclusiveness, its authoritative reach. Steven Zeitchick summed it up this way: "Indeed, what Coe has managed is the tricky feat of depicting the claustrophobia and vulnerability of youth without sacrificing larger political and cultural truths. He gets both the kids *and* the adults right."[14] *The Rotters' Club* was awarded the Bollinger Everyman Wodehouse Prize, the United Kingdom's only literary award specifically for comic writing. Coe, a dedicated reader of P. G. Wodehouse in youth, presumably was proud to win the award bearing his name.

The Rotters' Club is a free-standing novel, but it is also the first wing of a fictional diptych; a closing Author's Note reads, "There will be a sequel to *The Rotters' Club*, entitled *The Closed Circle*, resuming the story in the late 1990s" (403). This promised sequel appeared three years later, providing answers to the question of what happened to the characters depicted in *The Rotters' Club*. The answers are generally gloomy. Youthful hopes have been modified; expectations of a political renaissance have been dashed first by the Thatcher revolution and then by the compromised Labor government of Blair. The title refers both to government by insiders, that is, a repudiation of the open society, and to the circle readers met in the earlier book. The closure is something like a closing in, if not a closing down. Florence Noiville comments: "What is striking about Jonathan Coe's work, as is the case with his British colleagues [she is a French observer], is his fashion of anchoring his universal truths in the immediacy of contemporary society. One has the impression of glancing through the *Times* with one eye while reading a novel with the other in his recreation of four years of Blairism still so close to us (1999–2003)" (298). One way of placing these two novels in Coe's oeuvre is to think of them as his condition-of-England novels of the 1970s and 1990s, chronologically flanking *What a Carve Up!*, which is mostly about the 1980s, although there are significant tonal differences that complicate this view.

Also in 2004 Coe published *Like a Fiery Elephant*, his biography of the pioneering British experimentalist B. S. Johnson (called by reviewer Robert Winder "a one-man avant-garde"), whose fearless testing of the limits of fictional form accompanied a sad life ended early by suicide.[15] Johnson is clearly one of Coe's influences, on the more experimental side of his work. The biography was very well received, considered to supply a long-felt need, and received the very prestigious Samuel Johnson Prize, awarded each year for the best work of British nonfiction.

Coe's most recent novels are quite different from what readers might expect, either from the playful, metafictional combination of comedy and rage in *What a Carve Up!* and *The House of Sleep* or from the more social-realistic, panoramic, microcosm/macrocosm of the Trotter books.

The Rain Before It Falls has been called a "woman's book." Coe said in an interview at the time of publication that *The Rain Before It Falls* was "an *hommage*" to the important series of modern women's books, the Virago Modern Classics.[16] (He has also written introductions to two of these volumes, Rosamond

Lehmann's *Dusty Answer* and *The Echoing Grove.*) In character names he alludes to important female predecessors, Rosamond and Beatrix Lehmann and Ivy Compton-Burnett. The novel reveals what happens when a woman is named executrix of her aunt's estate and listens to recordings that are the aunt's last testament to an abandoned child and grandchild. As one reviewer, Toby Lichtig, wrote, what follows is "a tale of snowballing dysfunction hidden behind images of suburban calm and smiling faces. . . . Coe has a knack for capturing the psychological magnitude of tiny events."[17]

Not only has this novel moved from male to female central characters; not only has it eschewed "world-historical" events in favor of the equally moving account of little betrayals and meannesses; it lacks the political passion of some of his earlier books, except in the sense that the personal is the political. Or perhaps the ethical is the political. This book seems more grounded in ethical discriminations than its predecessors.

On his website, Coe explains what he was trying for with his 2010 novel, *The Terrible Privacy of Maxwell Sim:*

> I wanted it to be, among other things, a sort of British 'road movie', finding narrative interest in a journey along the M40, the A5192 and the A74(M)—names which always sound so prosaic alongside their glamorous American counterparts like Highway 61 or Route 66. In this respect, Lindsay Anderson's film *O Lucky Man!* was a big influence. I've always loved the way that film finds a kind of bleak visual poetry in Britain's motorway network. I was also inspired by Henry Fielding's two great picaresque novels, *Joseph Andrews* and *Tom Jones,* and the narrative energy they generate by sending their heroes on long journeys filled with random comic adventures.[18]

What a handsome summary this is of the way Coe's novelistic project interacts with popular culture (Route 66 would be glamorous in England only because it was the setting of a television show), film, and the English literary canon (recall that he wrote a doctoral dissertation on Fielding). Sim's plight, or predicament, is specifically contemporary, imprisoned by marital failure but further by the technology of portable telephones and GPS systems (Satnav, to the British)—he has his most intimate relationship with the voice of his Satnav. He bleakly illustrates one side of modern capitalism, too, in his doomed quest to travel the land selling a special kind of toothbrush. Like some of Coe's other characters he eventually comes to question not just his human worth but his gender affiliation, and this is seen not as an additional complication to his life but as a possible simplification he has been too blind to accept.

The Terribly Privacy of Maxwell Sim attracted a more mixed critical reaction than Coe usually receives, with some readers thinking that in his choice of satirical targets he had gone too much for the low-hanging fruit, although others, like Mark Sanderson in the *Sunday Telegraph,* thought it "brilliantly evokes the debilitating loneliness of complete isolation, how the mind can sabotage itself. . . . *The Terrible Privacy of Maxwell Sim* is . . . cunningly plotted, extremely well-written and very, very funny."[19]

In *Expo 58,* published in the autumn of 2013, Coe returned to his interest in mid-twentieth-century Britain and the European continental culture toward which it was edging. Set in the 1950s, it is a seriocomic look at that decade through a set of representative characters and a significant event. The title alludes to the World's Fair, or Exposition Universelle et Internationale, hosted by Brussels in 1958. As the novel explains, it was "held at a time of unprecedented optimism" about advances in nuclear science and about the possibilities of peaceful cooperation among nations.[20] The optimism is qualified or ironized both by lingering wartime privation and by international mistrust and misunderstanding. The novel is focused through Thomas Foley, a minor civil servant assigned to the British effort at the Expo and one of Coe's average men, never quite understanding his role, counterposed with large forces he only partly comprehends.

Clearly there is no fixed pattern in Coe's fiction that would permit a reader to predict what he will do next. After ten novels in twenty-six years, he is apparently at the peak of his powers. Although a committed writer who hopes to write a book every five years or so, he is also still interested in music and film (he wrote a script, not finally used, for a film version of *The Dwarves of Death.*) He has in fact added musical performance and collaboration to his portfolio, including *9th and 13th,* a musical adaptation of one of his handful of short stories. Coe also takes full advantage of modern digital forms of publication, with a well-maintained website and two digital books released so far: *Pentatonic: A Story of Music* (2102), which is a short story released both as an e-book and as an audio book with musical accompaniment by his collaborator Danny Manners, and *Marginal Notes, Doubtful Statements: Non-fiction, 1990–2013,* released in December 2013 as a Kindle book.

TWO

Early Novels

Jonathan Coe had been a precocious novelist, beginning with a short book he wrote when he was seven or eight years old, followed by others he wrote at eleven and fifteen (a James Bond imitation and a satirical novel that he actually sent to a publisher). He had written fiction while an undergraduate, and he wrote and submitted more during his postgraduate studies at Warwick. But his first published, as opposed to written, novel was *The Accidental Woman,* which appeared in 1987. He has explained the process of getting his book accepted: "I was posting manuscripts in a Jiffy bag with a Coventry postmark as a complete unknown. *The Accidental Woman* was the third or fourth novel submitted, having already received the usual 15 previous rejections."[1] It was eventually drawn from the slush pile by Anna Haycraft, who was the wife of and the fiction reader for Colin Haycraft at Duckworth, as well as a novelist herself under the name Alice Thomas Ellis. Coe received an advance of £200, and the book sold 272 copies in hardback.

It is a commonplace, and perhaps an exaggerated one, to expect that first novels will contain considerable autobiographical material. Certainly this is not the case for *The Accidental Woman* except, perhaps, for the area in which his protagonist Maria—like Coe—grows up, the Birmingham suburbs, and, as Philip Tew suggests, his university years: "Curiously Cambridge, where he completed his undergraduate degree, scarcely features, although perhaps his unenthusiastic opinion of the institution and ambivalent feelings toward that phase of his experience are transposed to Oxford where he situates the unhappy university education of Maria in his first novel, *An Accidental Woman*" (47). Other areas of his earlier life would appear in his next two novels: postgraduate study in *A Touch of Love,* rock music and band membership in *The Dwarves of Death.*

Much more influential on the novel were various authors Coe had been reading, whose names are surprising because of their difference from one another.

The most important ones were three twentieth-century writers: Flann O'Brien, the experimental Irish author; the British experimentalist B. S. Johnson, whose biography Coe would later write; and the Scottish Alasdair Gray. Alongside these were centuries-old predecessors: Henry Fielding (subject of his doctoral thesis) and Laurence Sterne. From Johnson he adopted the doctrine that the modern novel "should be Funny, Brutalist and Short"[2]; although this definition comes from Christie Malry, a fictional character in Johnson's novel, the author's resistance to fiction as "lying" makes it easy to identify the belief as Johnson's. To Fielding, perhaps, as well as to O'Brien, some credit may be due for his narrative approach, described by Coe as an "intrusive narrative subverting its conventional possibilities."[3]

The Accidental Woman is about Maria, the title character, and the life she leads between the ages of about seventeen and her early middle age, during which she attends university at Oxford, has several unsatisfactory affairs, marries and has a son, and is divorced. The critic Lidia Vianu calls Maria "a perplexing, deliberately unexplained (yet not at all enigmatic) heroine."[4] Vianu considers the lack of mystery about Maria to derive from Coe's disregard for suspense. However, it is not so much suspense—in the conventional sense of being required by the author to wait before finding out what will happen, while being made curious—that he disdains as much as the normal expectations of narrative and character. There is a certain amount of suspense in the plot, in the sense that readers do not know what will happen next (and there are occasional foreshadowings), but by the same token the suspense is nearly inert since the narrator is at such pains to assure us that nothing matters.

The tone of the novel is set early by such "intrusive" narratorial remarks as these: having introduced Maria and her long-time sad sack of a suitor, Ronny, he sums up: "So that's two clowns we have met already"; elsewhere the narrator suggests, "Here you are to imagine a short scene of family jubilation, I'm buggered if I can describe one."[5] *The Accidental Woman* is an exuberantly metafictional text: that is, in Patricia Waugh's definition, it is "fictional writing which self-consciously and systematically draws attention to its status as an artifact in order to pose questions about the relationship between fiction and reality."[6] The tone of these narrator's comments is similar to those of Johnson's narrator in *Christie Malry's Own Double Entry* in their knowing and sarcastic references to the novelist's procedures. Johnson thought of fiction as lying and was at pains to undermine any tendency toward suspension of disbelief, to an extent and with a fervor that Coe does not share, using, for instance, a reference to "Headlam and Lucy, perhaps the only other sympathetic characters in this novel so far" or "What Christie thought, however (and how privileged we are to be able to know it)."[7] As Waugh points out, "In providing a critique of their own methods of construction, such writings not only examine the fundamental structures of narrative fiction, they also explore the possible fictionality of the world outside the literary fictional text" (2). Johnson was much more exercised by the facticity of the novel—he insisted that the novel should be true, that "fiction" was lying—than about the fictionality of the world outside the text.

One of the more prolonged passages of narrative reluctance, or indifference, comes in this account of Maria's sexual affair with a fellow undergraduate at Oxford: "There is no need to give the details. Why describe all the gropings, the senseless fumbles and thrusts which this poor misguided couple executed upon each other on warm spring afternoons and clammy evenings? Why enumerate, in the hope of enlightening or perhaps even arousing the reader, the various gasps, kisses, groans, caresses, stains and clasps which characterize this ludicrous pantomime? Far better to forget, as Maria tried often and vainly to forget, the hours she had spent with this man in the flagging pursuit of a hazy gratification" (48–49).

The novel makes its mark both by what it says and what it only seems to say or implies. Among its possible themes are the unsatisfactory nature of life itself. The opening—"Take a birth. Any birth" (1)—seems to assert that Maria is a representative person rather than an unusually unfortunate one. Her parents are uncomprehending, her relations with her brother are unsatisfactory, she has great difficulty making friends; when she marries a man, without love, the results are miserable. She does occasionally derive pleasure from listening to music. Her one possible chance for happiness seems to occur at Oxford; having fallen in love with a fellow undergraduate, Stephen—although her love makes little difference in the course of her life, and she occasionally "wondered whether he found her unattractive, or whether he was homosexual, or frigid" (70)—she goes and sits outside his college for five hours, awaiting him; meanwhile he leaves the college by a different exit, returns hours later, packs his things and departs Oxford. When Maria returns home her flatmate tells her "a man rang" but left no number (78). Near the end of the novel, she is still brooding over this lost chance. When she eventually decides to "settle" and asks Ronny if he will marry her (after he has has been proposing to her for ten years), he stands her up at the registry office.

Maria can be a difficult object of sympathy, however, as she is herself deficient in most of the characteristics that are likely to ingratiate characters with readers (but not looks: the narrator mentions, late in the novel and in a sort of aside, that she is physically impressive). She has a very low-level family fondness, mostly for her cat. Although she considers conversation an overrated pastime, "occasionally she craved it, simply as a change from all the other overrated pastimes" (42). Even her more appealing traits are themselves subjected to a ruthlessly ironic examination by the narrator. She writes poetry, for instance: "Why Maria wrote these poems, what pleasure she took in wrestling with emotions, disguising them as thoughts and misrepresenting them in words, what satisfaction she derived from copying them out in a fair hand and reading them over to herself, I cannot say. Probably none" (6–7). Her disappointments and miseries make her an intolerant person and thus intolerable, and the narrator reveals that she is unpopular with, even hated by her neighbors—possibly because she depresses them—or possibly because she stands in supermarket queues uttering "soft cries" like "Puke and shit, puke and shit, day in, day out" (147).

Perhaps Maria is an exhibit, no better and no worse, in a novel the point of which is the unrelenting disappointingness of life. Some of the comments on issues larger than Maria's life suggest this reading: for instance, her flatmate Winifred "believed in the benevolence of God, the sanctity of marriage, and the innate goodness of human nature," an enumeration quickly followed up by "She was moronic in other ways, too" (58). One of these other ways is her determination to be kind and helpful to Maria. That Winifred later meets a man in the street while drunk and drugged and kills him with his own umbrella is another of the ironic or bathetic developments of Coe's plot.

It is hard to justify writing a novel, even a short one, to establish that an uninteresting life lacks interest, aside from the not very admirable fun possibly to be derived from snickering at Maria, or even to demonstrate some metaphysical proposition about life's implacable frustrations. More interesting is Coe's metafictional commentary on fiction itself. Chapter 2 begins with commentary on Maria's memories of Oxford, which the narrator identifies as false, but goes on to observe that "we might as well respect them, except perhaps for parts of the third chapter, where the mood will be rather more autumnal" (17). Elsewhere an account of a sad mistake Maria made—thinking she was listening to her love object Stephen playing the organ, when it was really his teacher—is introduced with "to tell the truth, never a bad thing to do occasionally even in a novel," and concluded with "her inaccurate memory meant much more to her than our knowledge of the facts can ever mean to us, so we needn't feel superior" (73). Much later, when Maria has gone to live in Chester, the narrator describes her habit of going into the Cathedral, where she kneels and hurls abuse at God, and the time she spends in the Garden of Remembrance: "What an opportunity for metaphor! Unfortunately we don't have the time" (141). Once the reader is told that it is time to "attempt a little characterization for a change" (108). There are ironic passages that satirize cliché: "How was she to know [when she agreed to marry Martin] that her fiancé would turn out to be, at the end of the day, and to be perfectly frank, and when all was said and done, a malignant shit, not to put too fine a point on it?" (105). There are ironic passages that satirize irony, as when one is introduced with "irony coming up" (73). And tense: the last chapter begins "It is one week later" (149) and continues with that convention, one often used in contemporary fiction to "bring the narrative up to date" or add "immediacy," until the narrator interjects, "Do you mind if we revert to the past tense? I find the other so exhausting" (150).

Beyond these "local" ironies about the practice of novel writing there is the larger issue of belief, commentary on which appears most openly when the narrator reveals that Maria's marriage results from a decision to eat gammon one afternoon (perhaps an example of her being an accidental woman). From an account of her misery, "a misery such that I cannot describe and you probably can't imagine, so we'd better just leave it" the narrative proceeds to this: "It is customary, of course, when it comes to stories like this, to believe whatever the author tells you, and yet I can imagine that for some of you there might be a problem in taking at face value my assertion in the first sentence of this chapter" (86). In his fluid combination of certainty about Maria—whose inner being he plumbs when convenient—and uncertainty about her thoughts or the meaning of her life, this narrator resembles Henry Fielding's narrator in *Joseph Andrews* and *Tom Jones,* who is likewise voluble and self-revealing and given to inviting the reader to share in the problems of narration: "The reader may imagine much better and quicker too than I can describe, the many embraces and tears of joy which succeeded her arrival"[8]—although invoking sympathy is contrary to what Coe is usually up to in *The Accidental Woman.* When Fielding's narrator sometimes claims to be unable to satisfy the reader on some question of fact, Coe's is more likely to decline on account of indifference or laziness: he can't be "buggered" to do it. He has referred to this as using the novel's "intrusive narrator subverting its conventional possibilities."[9]

It is important to acknowledge, finally, that this novel is funny. It is true that the plot is dreary and, to the extent that the reader sympathizes with Maria, sad. But there are many funny lines, often relying on surprise reversals of expectation, often ironically undermining romantic or other literary clichés. Such is the narrator's account of Maria's first night with her roommate at Oxford: "That first evening, they sat together by the fire, and talked long into the night. This gave rise to a spontaneous and mutual antipathy" (17). Maria's supervisor introduces a heartfelt conversation with this: "When one has been at Oxford for as long as I have, teaching, working for the university, and when one is married to a man who has also taught, and worked for the university, for a long while, then one is bound to have accumulated a certain amount of—how shall I put it?—money" (50). And then there is the summary of the "little gestures" that, according to one of Maria's female friends, trying to help her out with men, "render men helpless, turn them to putty in our hands." These are, "in ascending order of effectiveness, the fluttering of the eyelids, the crossing of the legs, and the sucking of the penis" (70–71).

It is probably this unexpected mixture of breezy humor, witty commentary on the very practices of the novel the reader has in hand, and a sometimes almost nihilistic presentation of the possibilities of human freedom, success, or happiness that makes this first novel so compelling. The last page demonstrates all these traits, as well as accident. Having gone to visit her family and tried unsuccessfully to get any of them to join her on her walk, Maria is at a park she remembers from childhood. A lark sings, and she returns its regard. "I find the thoughts of both, at this point, equally impossible to divine. It is even hard to say with which, of the two, I feel more in sympathy, but let us for the sake of this story cast our lot with the lark"; the narrative then proceeds to offer a literal bird's-eye view of Maria, concluding with her, as seen by the lark, as a "speck in the unseen, homeward bound, alone, and indifferent, indifferent even in the face of death which who knows may be the next thing chance has in store for her" (165).

Two years later came *A Touch of Love,* an academic novel centering on an unhappy postgraduate student at the University of Warwick (Coe's graduate school), located in Coventry. As Philip Tew writes, it shares with *The Accidental Woman* "its reflexive brevity, a notion of random causality and a mood of negativity" (48). A change in the narrative technique relocates some of these traits into interpolated narratives in the form of four short stories written by Robin Grant, the protagonist. Tew calls this a satirical campus novel, but this term seems inappropriate for a novel in which, although matriculated at a university, the characters seldom visit the university, in fact avoiding the more important aspects of campus life, such as interaction with tutors, going to the library, writing a thesis: in short, making perceptible academic progress. And, although there is satire, it is distributed, and readers may be uncertain what or who is its object.

The novel begins with the arrival in Coventry of a successful electronics salesman, Ted, who somewhat unwillingly visits his old Cambridge friend Robin in his grubby flat. The conversation between them amusingly reveals how differently they regard their shared past (only five years earlier), and it grows obvious that Robin's difficulty with Ted arises not just from the difference between them (Ted is obtuse, bluff, selfish, worldly) but also from Robin's love for Kate, Ted's wife. Robin reveals that he writes fiction and Ted reads one of his stories; he stays over and, before he goes, makes suggestions for Robin's amendment of his life. In the park, Robin goes into some bushes to urinate; this leads to his being charged with child molestation. He has a defense attorney who gradually loses interest in defending him; Ted, appealed to for an alibi, refuses to testify and suggests Robin is guilty. His short stories are read tendentiously as confirmation of his twisted sexuality. Near the end of the novel Robin visits Aparna, one of his few real friends, and ends by throwing himself from the balcony of her fourteenth-floor flat.

In an interview Coe told Philip Tew that "whenever I start a novel or even start thinking about a novel there are always crucial formal choices to be made, and . . . I never take the form of a novel for granted" (42). Formally, *A Touch of Love* is quite subtle. It is divided into four parts; each of them contains some narrative of Robin's life and one of his short stories, with different explanations of how they come to be read by others, and each of the parts is named for the short story it contains: these are "A Meeting of Minds," "The Lucky Man," "The Lovers' Quarrel," and "The Unlucky Man." The juxtaposition of the stories with events in Robin's life makes the stories themselves, as well as their titles, ironic commentary on the novel; thus, the meeting between Ted and Robin, who speak and think mostly at cross-purposes, is ironized by the chapter title "A Meeting of Minds," and the chapter "The Lucky Man" consists largely of legal discussion of Robin's having accidentally gotten himself charged with a sex crime. Chapters 1 and 3 take place on consecutive days in April 1986; chapter 2 takes place in July of the same year, after Robin has been charged, and chapter 4, on December 19, 1986, the last day of his life. There is a short postscript by Aparna dated October 1987. The nonchronological arrangement particularly of the first three chapters removes suspense, perhaps, but increases the dramatic irony of Robin and Ted's conversation in the park.

The narrative is, as in most of Coe's novels, heterodiegetic, that is, "third person" discourse from a narrator who is not a character, aside from Aparna's postscript, and so are Robin's stories. The "outside" narrator of *A Touch of Love* is free of the more showy qualities of self-display or self-reference seen in *An Accidental Woman,* but Robin's narrators are not, calling attention to themselves and their procedures with comments like "it would frankly bore the backside off the pair of us if I were to try describing them"[10] and "if we might undertake a bit of psychology at this point (it hasn't been the strong point of this story so far, I admit)" (110–111) and, with a less sarcastic but more skeptical blast against his own writing, "I dislike this mode of writing. You pretend to be transcribing your characters' thoughts (by what special gift of insight?) when in fact they are merely your own, thinly disguised. The device is feeble, transparent, and leads to all sorts of grammatical clumsiness. So I shall try to confine myself, in future, to honest (honest!) narrative" (34). This is another Johnsonesque explanation, comparable to the narrator's statement (to his character Christie) that "it does not seem to me possible to take this novel much further. I'm sorry."[11]

What is this story a story *of*? In one sense it is a satire on the life of a somewhat futile man, exacerbated by his involvement—also futile—in the postgraduate study of literature. In another it is a further examination of the role of chance and accident in dictating the course of a life. Perhaps there is also a suggestion of remedy for the futility and pathos of a life like Robin's.

In addition there is political anger. Coe has written that that he used as the novel's "focal point" Ronald Reagan's bombing raid on Libya in 1986, employing long-range bombers flying from U.S. bases in Britain.[12] The raid occurred on

April 14, 1986, and was retaliation for several acts of violence the United States blamed on the Libyan president Muammar Gaddafi, most proximately a bombing in a Berlin dance hall that seemed to target U.S. servicemen. In the United Kingdom the controversy arose from Prime Minister Margaret Thatcher's having given permission for bombers from bases in Britain to take part; by contrast, France, Spain, and Italy denied the United States Air Force permission to fly through their air space. The first page of the novel broaches the idea of a nuclear war, and Robin is greatly exercised by his outrage over this episode. Coe, too, considered that "a defining, apocalyptic historical moment" but on reflection considered that it had "very little resonance" in the book through his own failures as a novelist.[13] The reviewer John Lanchester concurred, saying that "the political background to the book, which makes the Libyan bombing a trigger for Robin's accidie, is well-meaning but unpersuasive."[14] The French reviewer Bruno Portesi seems to have found the politics more successful, calling Coe "par excellence l'écrivain de l'anti-thatchérisme."[15]

Philip Tew by contrast refers to *A Touch of Love* as Coe's "satirical campus novel" (48). There is indeed a critique of the stasis of the postgraduate student life. Some of this is focused on Hugh Fairchild, a man who both embodies and describes the condition of postgraduates. Four years after finishing his own degree he is idle. About Robin, he explains, "He often forgets to shave. He always smells like that. He's a student. Worse than that, he's a postgraduate student. What incentive is there to keep up appearances?" (56). He predicts, correctly, that Robin will never complete a thesis and comments prophetically, "If he were to start being realistic it would be disastrous. He'd realize that life had nothing in store for him any more. He'd probably kill himself" (60). Robin is himself quite aware, and in reveries of a future interview on a chat show, he discusses "the so-called Coventry group," contrasting them sarcastically with the Parisian intelligentsia in Montparnasse cafés; asked, in imagination, if the university played an important part in the group's intellectual life, he answers, "Yes, it did. It was where we used to buy our sandwiches"; asked for the main characteristics of the group, he responds, "Pallor, depression, extreme social gracelessness, malnutrition and sexual inexperience" (132–134). He goes on to discuss his own writing, dividing it into his creative writing—his stories, all of which are unpublished and most unread—and his literary criticism (that is, his thesis), which is not just unread but unwritten.

This part of the novel contains some levity, but it is less important than the investigation of why things happen as they do. Many details suggest a life driven by chance. The proximate cause of Robin's final despair is his having been charged with child molestation, and this happened because his friend Ted encouraged him to drink too much tea and to sit in a park, to the point that he needed to go into the bushes to relieve himself; by mere chance a boy kicked his football into the bushes, and this led to the charge. There are other coincidences that seem to indict randomness. And one of Robin's stories contains the fullest explanation of this world view: his character Lawrence in the story "The Lucky Man" describes his life as "a chain of accidents" (97); he goes on to insist that "Our so-called choices, these supposedly responsible decisions—ultimately they have to be made in the context of factors over which we have not the slightest control. Realize this, you see, and you are on the way to understanding life" (99). This belief gives him serenity, which differentiates him sharply from Robin.

The tragic, or at least pathetic, ending of Robin's life calls, perhaps, for some meaning. Near the end two remedies for such a plight as his are suggested, one of them thinking and the other love. Emma, Robin's defense attorney, says to Hugh, "start thinking, Hugh. A little New Year's resolution, maybe—for both of us. Let's both start thinking now" (224). That she has failed in his defense, in part through becoming entangled with Hugh, a perpetual student, might make readers question her standing, though. And Aparna thinks of saying to passersby, "You should think, think, think about what is happening all around you. Think until your heads hurt with the effort and the worry of it. Thinking is not always dangerous, you know. It killed Robin but it will not kill you" (231).

Hugh also reads Robin's last story, "The Unlucky Man," with Robin's comments, suggesting the inclusion of some words from Simone Weil's *Gravity and Grace* (a book, published in 1947 and in English translation in 1952, made up of excerpts from the journal of this French philosopher and mystic that makes an important appearance again in *The House of Sleep*); the most important quotation from Weil includes this: "When the 'I' is wounded from outside it starts by revolting in the most extreme and bitter manner like an animal at bay. But as soon as the 'I' is half dead, it wants to be finished off and allows itself to sink into unconsciousness. If it is then awakened by a touch of love there is sharp pain which results in anger and sometimes hatred for whoever has provoked this pain" (223–224). Hugh denies the relevance of the thinking of Weil, whom he dismisses as "some French woman" (223), to Robin's life or death, and the connection is not completely clear, but the echo of Weil's prose in the book's title, along with the nearly loveless texture of the novel, suggests that this may be Coe's diagnosis of Robin's "problem."

A Touch of Love shares with Coe's other early novels a feminist repulsion for violence against women and the men who perpetuate it. In *An Accidental Woman,* Maria's husband, Martin, beats her; he also favors violent sex, although, as the narrator ironically concedes, "it was rare for him actually to kick her in the face at such moments" (89). Tina, William's flatmate in Coe's third novel, *The Dwarves of Death,* is being punched and strangled by her boyfriend. Ted, in *A Touch of Love,* is not so brutal, although his thoughts about Kate reveal him as a controlling man and, in regard to one argument over where they should buy a vacation home, concluded in Ted's favor, the narrator chillingly reveals that "physical force had not been necessary after all" for Ted to get his way (13). His treatment of his wife makes Robin's unavailing (and always unspoken) love for her more moving, and her having married Ted rather than Robin comes to seem one more accident.

The Dwarves of Death marks a departure after the first two novels. It has a homodiegetic, that is, "first-person" narrator in the person of William, a keyboard player in a band. He is from Leeds and has come to London to be a musician, although with very modest success. Movement from Leeds to London and back at the end places this novel in the subgenre about the young man from the provinces, aligning it with classic novels like F. Scott Fitzgerald's *The Great Gatsby* (1925) and Stendhal's *The Red and the Black* (1830). Early on he offers an explanation for why he dislikes the music of Andrew Lloyd Webber: "for the same reason that I dislike London: because everybody else flocks to it as if it were the only thing worth experiencing on earth," and in the short coda, back in Leeds, he insists that "Anything beats London."[16] He plays in a band called The Unfortunates, an allusion (by Coe; not consciously by William) to a novel of the same name by B. S. Johnson; probably Johnson's most famous or infamous work, it consists of unbound sections in a box to be read in any order the reader prefers. William's band is made up of semiskilled players: "Our hold on the pathetically simple music we used to play remained as fragile as ever. It still wasn't unknown for us to lose time completely in the middle of a twelve-bar blues" (70–71). Although William has some serious jazz training, he shares the ambition of the rest of the band—"the holy grail which is the gleam in the eye of every aspiring band"—to make it in rock music (71).

The Dwarves of Death is much richer in plot than *The Accidental Woman* and *A Touch of Love* and qualifies as something of a thriller. It begins with William going to meet a man, at the behest of his manager, with whom he might have more musical success. William naively thinks, "I felt I'd reached some kind of turning point. . . . I would never have believed that things were going to get even worse" (3). In short order he witnesses a murder, seeing a man battered to death by two sinister dwarves in hoods. He then explains that he has begun with the difficult part and now plans to go back and explain the background, claiming that Andrew Lloyd Webber is to blame. This claim resembles the suggestion in *The Accidental Woman* that everything followed from eating gammon on a hot day and is another suggestion, like those in the first two novels, of the contingent nature of all human events. As William thinks, "What could I do? I had been on the point of giving them a complete explanation—of narrating a more fantastic chain of events than I could ever have invented, in the hope that they would believe me and find some way of helping me out. But I couldn't do that now. Once again, circumstances were sweeping me away, carrying me beyond the realm where decisions could be made and free will exercised" (178).

What follows is an extended flashback, consisting of 140 of the 214 pages in the book. The most important information provided has to do with William's frustrating love for a cold, indifferent woman named Madeline; his relationship with another woman, a barmaid named Karla; his background in Leeds and the girlfriend he had there; and his living situation in London. He lives south of the Thames in a grubby estate and shares a flat with yet another woman, whom he seldom meets because of their conflicting working hours but with whom he communicates by leaving notes. The most crucial of the women in William's life is Madeline, another of the icy beauties of Coe's fiction who are often unfortunately entangled with male characters who are ineffectual with women. (Another later instance is Cicely in *The Rotters' Club.*) Pamela Thurschwell is most interested in Coe's later books, but she points out that "Coe refuses to let his male fictional alter egos succeed via art; they can't write their way out of their historical predicaments, or break free of their arrested adolescences. They seem trapped by history and chained to early erotic fantasies."[17] She might have added that they have a still-youthful dedication to the musician's lifestyle, so, while they cannot write their way out of predicaments, they cannot escape through music, either. And they are no match for women like Madeline. As William reports on one of their dinner dates: "A swirl of feelings, compounded of desire and incipient affection and a wish to apologize, swept over me and it was all I could do to refrain from leaning across the table and kissing her long and gently on the mouth." When he does kiss her good night he "felt that no satisfaction could be more complete. Perhaps I would have been less happy if I had known that on this first date, Madeline and I had come as physically close as we would ever come; that we would never surpass that kiss—wouldn't even equal it, more often than not" (97).

Madeline cultivates an air of mystery that incorporates the comedy of miscommunication. When William is trying to discover more about a certain Piers she keeps mentioning, she says she used to have a man in her life, with whom she walked a dog on Hampstead Heath: "'What was his name?' 'Rover, I think. This food's a long time coming, isn't it?'" (96)

Returning to the night of the murder, Williams addresses the reader directly: "I'll try not to exaggerate, and I'll try to say exactly what I mean: and for your part, you must take these words and really think about them" (161). Events accelerate; he calls on Madeline and meets her new boyfriend—who, being Piers, seems to have been her boyfriend all along; he takes care of the son of some friends; and he finds out that his roommate Tina, who has been battered by her boyfriend, Pedro, partly through William's accidental failure to lock the flat one night, has taken an overdose. Eventually he gets a baroquely strange account from Karla explaining who the dwarves are and why they did the initial killing. He even witnesses a close-range shotgun murder and drops through a trap door into the Thames. There is a short coda back in Leeds, where a friend tells him he has grown up and he shares mild joking about Andrew Lloyd Webber. There is more, but this summary indicates how much more event-charged, how much more plot-rich this novel is than *The Accidental Woman* and *A Touch of Love.* William is not much more effectual in making things happen than Maria or Robin: like them, he is a person to whom things happen, but the life he leads is much more exciting. In fact it is too exciting, which helps to explain why he returns to Leeds at the end and to a more ordinary life.

After its two predecessors, *The Dwarves of Death* comes as a turn in a new direction. Whether that is a welcome change is debatable. William's voice is less interesting, less ironic, less knowing than the voices of the omniscient narrators of *A Touch of Love* or *The Accidental Woman* or even the narrators of Robin's short stories. He is earnest, well-meaning, a little naïve. He is believable but not terribly engaging. His discourse is not without humor, sometimes through wry deprecation of his band's abilities: he explains that his drummer, Jake, wrote songs "which combined the philosophical complexity of 'Bat Out Of Hell' with the raw rock'n'roll energy of Schopenhauer's *The World As Will and Representation*" (69–70). After this book, most of Coe's novels will have a detached heterodiegetic narrator, which is not to say that first-person voices will not be included, as many of his texts incorporate journals, letters, reminiscent articles, and so on, but these almost always (*The Terrible Privacy of Maxwell Sim* being the most notable exception) occur within a larger matrix in which the narrative tasks are not assigned to one of the characters. Coe is on record being, like B. S. Johnson, concerned with form in all his fiction, as is clear from his assurance, in an interview with Philip Tew quoted earlier, that thinking about form and his "crucial formal choices" is primary in his planning for any novel.

Reviewers had mixed reactions to *Dwarves;* for instance, Christina Koning spotted a debt to Martin Amis's *Money* in the combination of "thriller, downbeat love story and black comedy."[18] Jennifer Potter welcomed the "blackish" humor but complained of the very long flashback that "by the time Coe brings us up to date, the murder is all but forgotten and the belated introduction of 'clues' and 'explanations' is as dissonant as William's band."[19] The esteemed critic Julian Symons reviewed it with three other books but concluded that it is "a lively and likeable novel."[20] A French reviewer, Corinne Le Dour-Zana, coming to it after *What a Carve Up!* had made Coe famous, found it less forceful than *Testament à l'anglaise* (the French title for *What a Carve Up!*) but still "inspiré et généralement hilarant."[21] This suggests what Coe may have had in mind when, asked why his novels are so successful in France, he replied, "I can only go on what I'm told by French journalists: that they feel rather starved of novels which feature strong narratives, humour, and engagement with contemporary social issues."[22]

Coe's next novel, *What a Carve Up!*, excelled in all those qualities, perhaps most significantly the engagement with social issues, but before that novel appeared he had turned his hand to more extended nonfiction work.

THREE

Short Fiction and Nonfiction

Although Jonathan Coe is primarily and preeminently a novelist, his work in other forms, particularly nonfiction criticism and biography, is surprisingly copious and accomplished. In 2008 Coe told interviewers Francois Gallix and Vanessa Guignery that "I cannot write short stories."[1] This is not quite true, as he has published three short stories. His very slender output of short stories appeared in a slim volume called *9th & 13th,* published in 2005; in the introduction he acknowledges the scantiness of his output in that form, explaining that "I don't find it easy to write over a short distance, being drawn to complexity and panorama in fiction."[2] The three stories are "Ivy and Her Nonsense," "9th & 13th," and "V.O." Coe's modesty is not misplaced, although the stories are all competent and suggestive of larger themes and devices in his longer work.

"Ivy and Her Nonsense" is framed by a visit the narrator and his sister Gill make to the home of their dead grandparents, during which Gill sees their ghosts in a churchyard. The narrator then thinks back to his own ghostly vision during a Christmas visit to the grandparents. Having become excited by his grandmother's account of a man's murder by his wife (his grandmother was a member of the jury), he enters his grandparents' room to see a man next to his grandmother on the bed raising a knife. The rational explanation offered by his older sister is that he was wrapping their Christmas present, although some of the details do not work out. The narrator closes by praying to his "newly acquired God" (28). The setting is the Birmingham area of Coe's childhood, the region that figures again and again in his fiction, and the story is something of a tribute to his grandfather James Kay, to whom the short book is dedicated. Kay was the figure in Coe's childhood who most influenced him as a reader.

"9th and 13th" is set in New York and, with the opening "I live on the corner of 9th and 13th," seems to name a location, but the numbers soon develop into a metaphor about a chord on the piano, the narrator being a pianist; there is some suggestion that he is William, the keyboardist from *Dwarves of Death.*

He describes the chord in some detail, saying that it is "aching to resolve, to settle on something," and concludes "9th and 13th. The sound of possibility" (21). The story that follows is of a woman in his bar asking him to suggest a place to spend the night. He spins out a counterfactual story in which she stays with him and they fall in love and marry and have two children; he then reveals that he rebuffed her interest and never saw her again, concluding: "I don't know what chord I should play next. I can't decide" (28). The musical metaphor works well here, with the double significance of "resolve."

The third story, "V.O.," is the sharpest. In it a composer of film scores, William, is on the jury at the Fourteenth Annual Festival of Horror and Fantasy Cinema, occurring somewhere like (but not the same as) Cannes. He has a flirtation with a journalist, more serious to her than to him (he has a family back home); this reminds him of a similar relationship with a German writer, whom he had earlier led on, only now to discover that her film will be shown at the festival in "V.O." or "version original," requiring translators for those who do not know French, the language of the subtitles. The spurned journalist provides his translation, and, since the film is based on his affair with the filmmaker, many of the lines translated by Pascale have a searing relevance to their own relationship. The film is in German; the subtitles, in French, are then translated into English by Pascale, his former lover: "'*Bitte, kehr in deine Heimat zurück. Dort wirst du glücklicher sein. Manfred, kehr zurück.*' *S'il te plaît, retournes d'où tu viens. Tu y seras plus heureux. Retournes-y, Manfred.* 'Please go back to where you belong. You will be happier there. Go back, William.' He turned towards her abruptly, and said, 'The character's name is Manfred, isn't it?' But Pascale did not answer. All he could see were her eyes, shining in the dark" (43).

The story contains both satire and a simultaneous defense of lowbrow films. William insists that genre films can be artistically serious and continues: "It doesn't do to be snobbish about these things. Horror films don't tend to be taken seriously by critics but if you look at many of the entries at this festival, you'll find that they are very finely crafted works of art—the works of real *auteurs,* real visionaries" (31). The news that the next film is *Mutant Autopsy 3* highlights the bathos of his words. Other films include an American entry, *Vampire Brainsuckers Get Naked,* and there is some critique of the Quentin Tarentino school of filmmaking.

The final item in *9th & 13th* is called "Diary of an Obsession," an account of Coe's love for a Billy Wilder film called *The Private Life of Sherlock Holmes.* His love for the film is also linked to his grandfather, who introduced him to Sherlock Holmes stories. As he explains, "this film has become, for me, intimately bound up with ideas of loss: lost time, lost opportunities, the rapidity with which events recede into the past" (50). Along with an account of his efforts to recapture the film, there is an important link to his 1997 novel *The House of Sleep,* in which he invents a film critic who is obsessed with a lost Italian neorealist film. Coe shows how, even if subtly, that book pays tribute to the object of his obsession: that "novel contains only fleeting reference to *The Private Life of Sherlock Holmes,* but for those few people who love the film as I do, there is also a hidden network of codes and allusions. Ashdown, the name of my Gothic mansion, is also a name Holmes assumes in the film when he pretends to be a married man; Valladon, the name of the café where all the characters meet, is also the assumed name of the German spy with whom Holmes falls in love. And so on" (52).

"Diary of an Obsession" had been commissioned by *Cahiers du Cinema* and had never been published in English before; "Ivy and Her Nonsense" exists in a tiny chapbook published by Penguin in 1995; and "V.O" appears in *New Writing 7,* an anthology edited by Carmen Callil and Craig Raine and published in 1998.

Coe's own film criticism exists in a review of the film *The Madness of King George,* published in 2001, in which he examines the representation of insanity in film, comparing the film under review unfavorably with director Miloš Forman's 1975 *One Flew over the Cuckoo's Nest.*[3] There is a two-page article called "Hammer's Cozy Violence" in *Sight and Sound* from 1996.[4] Autobiography may be found in his introductions, in some of the entries on his website, and in a book called *Mortification: Writers' Stories of Their Public Shame,* in which he details some embarrassments occasioned by public readings from his work, none of them really very serious.[5]

A much greater volume of nonfiction writing comprises Coe's book reviewing. The introduction to *9th & 13th* expresses disdain for this body of work ("obscurity is exactly what most of that writing does deserve" [1]), but he is an incisive, humane, and well-informed critic. His best venue seems to have been the *London Review of Books,* which allows for much more expansive reviews than the daily newspapers, but he also has made significant contributions to the *Guardian* and the *Observer.* To appreciate his fiction it is not necessary to read his criticism. But doing so highlights some of his ongoing interests, which include biography; contemporary fiction, including experimental work and not limited by geography; popular culture, including film, television, and comedy; and some recurrent areas, such as the novels of Alasdair Gray. Asked by William May, in 2006, what impact his book reviewing had on his novel writing, he disavowed any important impact and said that he regarded the two "as completely independent activities," although he went on to say that reviewing had given him a good idea of what books were being published and thus "might have had a small part to play in inspiring me to write *What a Carve Up!* It would be too cynical to say that I saw a gap in the market, but I was aware that there hadn't been too many big, ambitious novels yet about the Thatcherite revolution, and perhaps that made me more inclined to attempt one."[6]

Writing in 1938, when it was possible for a person to make a living purely as book reviewer, Cyril Connolly strongly discouraged writers who wished to write books of lasting value from pursuing this profession (he suggested having a private income): "any other way of making money would be better . . . reviewing is a whole-time job with a half-time salary, a job in which the best in him is generally expended on the mediocre in others. . . . The sight of his friends' books accumulating depresses him and he knows that, besides losing the time to write books of his own, he is also losing the energy and the application, frittering it away on tripe."[7]

Jonathan Coe, by contrast, seems not to have damaged his career in any way by being a frequent book reviewer, and perhaps (in addition to any suggesting the opportunity for a satire on Thatcherism) reading many contemporary novels for review may have sharpened his awareness of his own approach and techniques.

Contributions to both the *Times* and the *Sunday Times* shed much light on his attitude toward comedy. Writing in 2009 in a piece called "What's So Funny about the British?," he gives a short history of British humor, beginning with the radio program *The Goon Show,* from the 1950s, and continuing with *Beyond the Fringe* (1960) and *That Was the Week That Was* (1962–1963) and concluding with contemporary satirists.[8] In "Low Culture Rises above Its Critics," a long feature from 1994, Coe gives his most vehement defense of popular culture, along with a barbed diagnosis of what ails the novel. He attributes to others a widespread belief that "what passes for 'high' culture in Britain today—the literary novel, the serious play, the art movie—has grown terminally inert and listless; popular culture is where it's at," but aligns himself with that view, at least partly, when he compares the impact on the public imagination of television or music with that of fiction. The contemporary equivalents of Tom Jones and Oliver Twist, he claims, are Inspector Morse and Basil Fawlty, and no play or British film has given him the pleasure to be derived from an album by the Beatles or the Smiths.

As for fiction, his own field, he complains that no contemporary writers are carrying on the tradition of B. S. Johnson, in Britain, or of Umberto Eco, Milan Kundera, Italo Calvino, or other continental masters. The key sentence contains his impression that "the majority of literary novels being published here at the moment, while full of intelligent ideas and in general very accomplished stylistically, are none the less weak on plot, weak on character and shy of formal innovation: somehow, it would seem we have evolved a brand of novel that contrives at once to be both middlebrow and deeply, irredeemably unpopular. As a result, the literary novel is now at the very margins of cultural life in Britain."[9]

He goes on to celebrate many British accomplishments in the popular arts and stipulates that the most significant of them are in comedy. Coe has often explained that he does not choose to write without comedy; humorlessness is a frequent complaint about the contemporary literary novel.

One extended article in a scholarly periodical—which on examination proves to be the transcript of a Laurence Sterne Memorial lecture delivered in 2004—appears as "'Great Spunky Unflincher': Laurence Sterne, B S Johnson, and Me" in the *Shandean,* a journal dedicated to Sterne studies. It repeats the connection between Johnson and Sterne in forming the kind of fiction Coe has chosen to write (the "great spunky unflincher" is Johnson's characterization of Sterne), while distinguishing them, again on the basis of humor. He quotes Tom Stoppard, who wrote that he saw no connection between *Travelling People* (Johnson's first novel) and *Tristram Shandy* "except that Sterne does certain things as marvelous, irrelevant and irreverent jokes . . . which Johnson does in grim meaningful earnestness."[10] This is a salutary reminder of one very important difference between Coe and Johnson, which may help to explain both Coe's much greater critical and popular success and his apparently happier life.

Another kind of nonfiction writing Coe has done from time to time comprises prefaces and introductions to other people's books. Two of these are reprinted work by B. S. Johnson. In 1999 Johnson's most famous (although probably not most widely read) book, *The Unfortunates,* was republished by Panther Books, and Coe provided the introduction, in which he told about Johnson's life, the aims of his writing, and the misery of his perceived failure and called for a Johnson revival.[11] *The Unfortunates* was one of Johnson's experimental "solutions" to narrative problems; it came in twenty-seven unbound sections, of which the first and last were identified as such while the reader was invited to read the others in any order at all. The sections came in a box. The aim, Coe explains, was to "convey the mind's randomness" (x). Some of Johnson's shorter work appeared in 2013 in a collection, this time edited by Coe among others, called *Well Done God! Selected Prose and Drama of B. S. Johnson.* In his preface Coe explains the reason for its publication and expresses satisfaction that most—but not all—of Johnson's work had been brought back into print.[12]

Another of his literary models, very different from B. S. Johnson or Samuel Beckett, was Rosamond Lehmann (1901–1990), and he contributed introductions, in 1996, to two of her novels then being reprinted: *Dusty Answer* and *The Echoing Grove.* He praises *Dusty Answer* for its gendered quality and for its accomplished portrayal of men and for the "thickly concentrated mixture of embarrassment and pleasure" that it associates with adolescence.[13] *The Echoing Grove* has entirely different strengths (and weaknesses, readily acknowledged): he ends by calling it "a visionary novel."[14] As in his other introductions, he smoothly combines the relevant biographical information with the artistic context of the work and what he takes to be its claims on a contemporary reader's attention. Some of the interest in his prefaces to these books derives from the knowledge that he has acknowledged Lehmann as a strong influence on his own fiction, particularly in *The Rain Before It Falls.*

Quite unlike Johnson or Lehmann is actress Shirley Eaton, for whose autobiographical *Golden Girl* Coe somewhat unexpectedly wrote the introduction. The title alludes to her role in the James Bond film *Goldfinger,* although Coe is clearly more interested in *What a Carve Up!,* in which she played a young nurse, the sex interest in the spoof horror film. Coe's introduction is short and almost perfunctory, although ardent in its praise of Eaton. Coe's readers will be more interested, perhaps, in Shirley Eaton's reaction to the use he made of her in *What a Carve Up!* She was given an advance copy of what she calls his "brilliant novel" and was uneasy at first, "but when I got used to Jonathan's freewheeling, wideranging, effervescent style, I began to like the book very much indeed."[15] She goes on to say that they had become friends, and he was an adviser to her on her own writing.

Finally, there is Jonathan Coe the biographer. He is the author of three full-length biographies, which vary widely. The first two are books about Hollywood actors, written (he has said) to support himself while he worked on a longer, more ambitious novel, more panoramic, richer, and deeper than his early books, that became *What a Carve Up!*[16] Whatever the motives of their composition, even these two are of keen interest because they testify to Coe's continuing interest in the cinema and, within that interest, in popular rather than just art films.

Humphrey Bogart: Take It and Like It was published in 1991 in both the United States and the United Kingdom In some ways it is a standard biography of a famous actor, illustrated with many photographs, working chronologically through the films and the life. But it has a sharp personal thesis that gives it rhetorical vigor. That thesis is indicated in the subtitle, a quotation from one of Bogart's lines in *The Maltese Falcon:* "Take it and like it." Coe first uses it to characterize the attitude of the studio bosses who controlled Bogart's career, indifferent to the quality of the films he made (at one stretch twenty-nine films in five years). But it also applies to Bogart, as when Coe refers to "the randomness and chance element in a life that in some ways got luckier as he got older."[17] Bogart is never portrayed as the Accidental Man, but Coe is, here as elsewhere, alive to the role of accident in any life. He has already generalized that "we are all of us engaged in life-long battles against authority, fought in the full knowledge that we live at the mercy of influences outside our control" (8); this belief helps to shape his account of Bogart's biography.

His analyses of Bogart's movies are clear and helpful. About the life, although not obviously opinionated, he is not uncritical, writing, for instance, about the famous marriage that grew out of *To Have and Have Not,* that "there was surely never a marriage that had so much grounding in the cinema, and so little in real life, as that between Bogart and Lauren Bacall" (97). This leads on to an incisive discussion of feminism, insisting that the American director Howard Hawks can hardly be considered a feminist, although he earned that reputation from some people because he favored strong women: Coe insists that Hawks's "strong women" were women who acted like men, which is why Bacall was encouraged to be as insolent as Bogart.

In addition to the pleasure provided by Coe's intelligent and discriminating criticism, the book pleases by its wit. On one page, the author informs readers that *Isle of Fury,* a 1936 adventure movie, "was the only film in which he ever got to wrestle with an octopus" and, in a caption to a still from that movie, reveals that "Bogart never gave a good performance while wearing a mustache" (32). Bogart's life, like most lives perhaps, declines from its peak, and Coe is good on the decline in his acting career as well as his terrible suffering from esophageal cancer. There is something, if not tragic, at least dignified and sad about the conclusion, in which he notes the brevity of the actor's real success: "fifteen years at the height of his profession, after more than four decades of struggles, setbacks, false starts, miscalculations, failed marriages, failed films, frustration, unhappiness" (190). Still, he insists, there is a recognizable "Bogart movie," comparable to a woman's movie. And he then widens the scope to supply a message: "if his career and his films provide equal cause for celebration, it is because they teach us a strategy, and a very wholesome one, for dealing with life at its best and its worst. Take it and like it" (190). This motto, with its mixture of toughness and existential stoicism, makes a good summary of his understanding of Bogart.

Three years later, *Jimmy Stewart: A Wonderful Life* appeared, from a different publisher but looking very much like a companion volume to the Bogart book. This is in some ways a less interesting book, because Coe is less interested in Stewart than in Bogart. He works hard at explaining Stewart's appeal and gives him full marks for earnestness and hard work, as well as for his impressive record in the Second World War. But he has trouble finding a significant central idea, as he had in the Bogart book, to help organize his text. There is the promising statement in the introduction that "much of that love [for a man he calls America's most beloved man] continues to centre upon a myth—upon the figure of the incorruptible American patriot, a part that Stewart in fact played only a handful of times and which is crystallised in a film now more than fifty years old"—that is, *Mr. Smith Goes to Washington.*[18] And he is alert to contrarian details, films in which Stewart plays sinister figures. But much of the satisfaction of reading this book comes from Coe's pungent critical judgments, for instance, that "the only one of his films to do lasting harm in the political arena was *The Stratton Story,*" since his being cast instead of Ronald Reagan freed Reagan to enter into politics (10)—and into history, including the bombing of Libya, which plays an important role in *A Touch of Love.*

He is equally vivid on Stewart's lesser-known films and on his most famous roles. He calls *Navy Blue and Gold* "a noxious conflation of the service academy/football film genres" (35) and diagnoses the "tendency to idealise him as the bumbling, guileless, essentially neutered country boy that rules out any real possibility of dramatic interest in . . . *The Shopworn Angel*" (41). He chuckles over Stewart's role in *How the West Was Won:* "The lack of conviction this lifelong Presbyterian brings to the role of long-haired reprobate is quite woeful" (172). But of the Oscar-winning *You Can't Take It with You* he writes "there can be few ordeals more grisly than having to sit through the complete film today" (44) and in what is Stewart's most lasting film he recognizes a disturbing counternarrative, commenting, "Take away its implausible resolution and sugar-coating of supernatural whimsy, and *It's a Wonderful Life* offers a vision of small-town life as explicitly disturbing as anything in the work of David Lynch" (86). Coe's identification of this subversive counternarrative renders that sentimental favorite more complex and intriguing.

As in *Humphrey Bogart,* Coe devotes some attention to gender relations, pointing out the "anti-feminist undercurrent" in *The Philadelphia Story* while acknowledging that "it would take a particularly humourless ideologue not to enjoy" that film's brilliance (69). By comparison with the Bogart volume, and perhaps in common with other biographers of living subjects, he has a bit more difficulty providing a strong ending for his book. Stewart was still alive at the time of writing (he would not die until 1997). A slowing of his acting career occurred not because audiences had turned against him. As Coe explains, his choices became backward-looking. His films "gestured back towards, or in some way tried to reclaim, a chimerical 'Golden Age' of Hollywood cinema in which Stewart's conservative, old-fashioned values had once flourished. And his pursuit of this mirage through the desert of 1970s permissiveness would lead him, eventually, to become involved with projects that can only be described as surreal" (184).

These include a Lassie movie, "an extraordinary musical farrago which required not only Stewart but even the dog to burst into song":

> Finally, in what has to be one of the most bizarre codas to any Hollywood career (let alone one as distinguished as Stewart's), his last commercially released feature film was a Japanese production, *Afurika Monogatari,* shot on location in Kenya in 1979. His character has only a handful of lines and is not even given a name, while on a technical level the film is barely competent, consisting almost entirely of footage of the local wildlife interspersed with meaningless fragments of dialogue. At the end of the move, the bearded Stewart pegs out on the floor of his hut and is buried by his granddaughter. And on this peculiar note, the cinema career of James Stewart comes to an end. (185)

So, despite what seems a less confirmed interest in his subject than was evident in the first film biography and a subject whose life and career resist treatment as a brave existentialist response to indifferent or hostile conditions, *James Stewart: A Wonderful Life* is a rewarding read because of its author's skill and personality.

Jonathan Coe's third biography is an entirely different kind of book. In a 2008 interview he commented on this difference. After expressing some embarrassment in talking about the two film-star biographies because they were commercial projects written for money and expressing a preference for the Jimmy Stewart book as more stimulating to write, he says: "But B. S. Johnson was completely different because nobody had a nice set of photographs of B. S. Johnson or wanted to give me a lot of money to write about him, and I had to work quite hard to persuade the publishers that a biography of B. S. Johnson was a good idea. But he was a writer that I had been very interested in since I had first discovered him in 1983 or 1984."[19]

He goes on to explain that his own introduction to Johnson was almost accidental. He had bought a copy of *Christy Malry's Own Double Entry* because it had a blurb by Samuel Beckett (which, interestingly, Johnson had used without authorization from Beckett, arousing Beckett's abiding anger) and came to understand that "I had stumbled upon a very unusual and interesting British writer, a writer who in many ways was violently at odds with the British literary establishment and with the British way of writing novels and thinking about novels. An unapologetic modernist who wants to experiment with form . . ." (41). In one of several passages in the book that explain Coe's (not completely unqualified) admiration for Johnson, he writes that "Few other writers, either during Johnson's lifetime or subsequently, have thought so hard about the novel as a form, have been prepared to put its possibilities to such intelligent scrutiny. Here perhaps is one working definition of 'writing as though it mattered.'"[20]

Having suggested to a publisher a book about Johnson's fiction, he was persuaded to write a biography instead (he maintains that the British love biography but not ideas). "I signed up to do a biography which I still thought would be a fairly short and simple book because my books about James Stewart and Humphrey Bogart had been fairly short and simple"—and because Johnson's life was short, his suicide coming when he was forty. But "in the end it turned into a very big book and it also turned into a very personal and I hope passionate book about writing and why people write and what people want to achieve by writing, for themselves."[21]

Published in 2005, *Like a Fiery Elephant: The Story of B. S. Johnson* took eight years to research and write. And, as we have seen, B. S. Johnson was very influential on Coe's career as a novelist: a model of artistic integrity (sometimes shading over into rebarbative stubbornness or rudeness), he was also, as Coe calls him, "Britain's one-man literary avant-garde of the 1960s" (3). The introduction to *Fiery Elephant* begins with an account of the young Coe, on holiday with his family, watching a 1974 broadcast called *Fat Man on a Beach,* more or less accidentally. (This motif, of an important childhood viewing of a film or television show affecting later life, reappears in *What a Carve Up!, The Rotters' Club,* and *The Terrible Privacy of Maxwell Sim.*) This featured B. S. Johnson: shown in November 1974, it was a film about a dead man, as Johnson had died in 1973. Ten years later, Coe goes on to explain, "I fell powerfully under his spell. I had emerged from the experience of reading English at Cambridge only lightly scathed and imbued with a thriving, unshakeable contempt for anyone who had had the temerity to attempt the writing of literature in the last seventy or eighty years" (5). His chance encounter with *Christie Malry's Own Double-Entry* having reintroduced him to Johnson, he soon came to accept some of Johnson's strongly held and even more strongly voiced ideas about modern literature: that the contemporary British novel was old-fashioned and hopeless because it had deviated from the modernist course set by Joyce and Beckett.

He seems never to have accepted Johnson's odd insistence that narrative curiosity is, in Johnson's words, "that primitive, vulgar and idle curiosity of the reader to know 'what happens next'" (6) or that fiction is a lie ("Telling stories really is telling lies" [35]) and that novels must tell the truth (rather puritanically defined). He does reveal some related questions about how or whether *non*fiction can tell the truth: "How, then, can a biography be anything other than one big lie, from start to finish? If (as I have discovered) even to condense the details of a comparatively short life such as B. S. Johnson's into five hundred pages requires grotesque, enormous acts of compression and selection, what hope is there for the whole enterprise?" (35). Recognizing the astringency of Johnson's own demands for truth telling, he responds, "writing itself becomes simply impossible if you subject it to standards like that. Better to go to the other extreme: no pretence of inclusiveness, no aspirations toward objectivity" (35). This helps to explain the presentation of the work as a set of fragments and the often very personal—that is, defiantly not objective—passages about Coe, including his own birth.

Nor has Coe taken up the pugnacious, uncompromising stance toward the reading public and his publishers that Johnson did: a refusal to change anything in his novels, a vociferous disdain for almost all other writers, accompanied by a fierce demand that he be compensated well for writing, largely irrespective of the literary marketplace. He was offensively demanding toward publishers about advances, rarely earned back by book sales, and for a while proposed being paid a substantial salary so he could write without worrying about the marketplace. He also expected his agent to find buyers for his poetry, plays, and television scripts as well as his fiction. Johnson's difficulties with publishers were related to his identification as a member of the working classes and a man of the left, with a strong labor-union conviction (Coe is from a different class but shares Johnson's left orientation). Through his short working life he wrote television screenplays and dramas for the stage as well as a great deal of journalism, including sports coverage, to support himself and his family, not very well.

Like a Fiery Elephant is a wonderful biography: intelligently discriminating, thorough, sympathetic, but with appropriate critical distance. Reviewers praised it: Julian Evans called it a "marvelous book"; Anthony Thwaite (abused by Johnson in life, as the biography reveals) called it "a biographical study which is much more impressive than anything produced by Johnson himself"; and Robert Winder raved: "It might even be possible that this biography is the book B. S Johnson was born to write—the vindication of his life and the climax of his career. It is earnest, dazzling, elegant, full of perceptions and, most important of all, true (especially when it comes to acknowledging the limits of what we can ever know)."[22] Some reviewers commented on the importance of Coe's own fiction: Rachel Cooke called *Like a Fiery Elephant* "a book about a man who really cares about novels, by a man who really cares about novels": Frank Kermode, in a long retrospective review-essay taking in Coe's biography and Johnson's novels, concluded by calling Coe "a conscientious but temporary biographer, who can now get on with his novels."[23]

Like a Fiery Elephant won the Samuel Johnson Prize for Nonfiction in 2005. Described (by its managers, although probably correctly) as "the UK's most prestigious non-fiction award," the Samuel Johnson prize was formerly underwritten by BBC channel 4 and is currently funded by an anonymous donor and administered by a steering committee. Coe's book won out over a shortlist that included other biographies, books about Bombay and Istanbul, and a history of nineteenth-century murder and grave-robbing. His prize was worth £30,000. The chair of the judging panel, Sue McGregor, acknowledged the difficulty of the subject, an author for whom empathy can be difficult to earn—but was achieved—and the "experimental style" of the biography, comparable to Johnson's own experimentalism.[24] Near the end of *Christie Malry's Own Double-Entry,* where the author himself appears to converse with his fictional character Christie, Johnson expresses dissatisfaction with fiction; when Christie asks him, "Your work has been a continuous dialogue with form?" he responds, "If you like."[25] For *Like a Fiery Elephant* Coe invented a new form for the biography. He told William May that he had written a quarter of the book in a conventional form but was dissatisfied with his failure to create a lucid narrative path: "I realized that writing a biography (or this biography) was formally not so very different from writing a novel, and at that point the writing became much easier and more fluid" (66).

What is that form? The table of contents announces an introduction, followed by three sections of unequal size: "A Life in Seven Novels"; "A Life in 160 Fragments"; and "A Life in 44 Voices." The introduction is subtitled, with some apparent facetiousness, "The Industrious Biographer: An Exposition Without Which You Might Have Felt Unhappy," and it explains the origins of Coe's interest in Johnson. The next section gives brief, one- to two-page introductions to Johnson's seven published novels. The central and most important section is the document-based narrative of Johnson's life, "A Life in 160 Fragments"; here, Coe explains, the important thing is not chronology (although chronology is clearly maintained by providing enough dates to keep the reader situated) but giving an impression of the subject's life, and therefore Coe will not attempt to exercise too much control over the "pile of material I've accumulated while writing this book"—"interview transcripts, conversations with the people who knew him best" (35), and forty boxes of Johnson's own papers made available by his widow, Virginia. The "fragments" consist of extracts from Johnson's diary, bits of letters to and from the author, poems, notes he made for his novels. They are connected by Coe's own prose.

The narrative voice is personal, sometimes with a knowing, jokey quality possibly reminiscent of Johnson, but even more of Coe's early novels: for instance, "If I were to write a novel about B. S. Johnson (and perhaps that's what I should have done instead, it sometimes occurs to me)" (64) or "You'll be pleased to learn that now, at last, things are going to start looking up for our hero!" (111). In some ways this biography of another man is more openly autobiographical than any of Coe's novels.

> I am writing these words in a tiny octagonal eighteenth-century building called the Bath House, which I have rented for this very purpose, for three days only, from the Landmark Trust. It stands a few miles from Stratford-upon-Avon and as I write I have a fine view over Warwickshire fields. Somehow it seems an appropriate place: various lines appear to converge at this point. It was built in 1748, the year of publication of Fielding's *Tom Jones,* my favourite novel. A few miles to the north lies Warwick University, where I wrote my thesis on *Tom Jones* in the 1980s and where I discovered Johnson's work. A few miles to the south are the Rollright Stones, where Johnson sat one Sunday afternoon in October 1961 and nibbled some toadstools and ate two scones which had been baked for him by Michael Bannard's mother. (376)

More somberly, he begins the last stage of the story, leading to the despairing Johnson's suicide, with a digression that tells the history of his writing the book, mentioning the novels he has completed and his children who had been born during its development, and acknowledges the difficulty of writing "the narrative of a man's death, in a few pages. . . . I have even started to feel—obliquely, vicariously, at thirty years' distance—some of the same anger and bewilderment that they [his family and friends] felt at the time. How can this be done? How can these pages be written?" (375).

Such stark reflections are intercut with some humor. Coe's comments on some of Johnson's work have the amusing asperity of his summaries of James Stewart's lesser films. Criticizing Johnson's last film made for the BBC, a documentary about Peter and Alison Smithson, architects whom Johnson admired extravagantly, he calls it a "positively eerie experience": "Never can late '60s fashions have looked so eccentric, for one thing. Sitting upright at what seems to be a kitchen table in extreme close-up, reading from cue cards with all the expressive variety of a dalek with a PhD, Alison Smithson appears to be wearing a child's spacesuit improvised out of tin foil for much of the film. The effect is frankly terrifying, and it's frequently hard to concentrate on what either of them is saying" (285).

The third section, "A Life in 44 Voices," consists of quotations from people who knew Johnson. As one would expect, they differ in their judgment of the man; two consecutive voices discuss the effect of drinking on the writer, the first noting that when he drank, "he never misbehaved himself under the influence of drink. He just got mellower and mellower, really—more and more genial," followed immediately by the observation that "he drank a great deal, and this is another factor of great importance: he became very angry and bitter through drink" (403). Two people suggest closeted homosexuality. The most insistent note is of a man who somehow sabotaged himself: one of his friends writes, "If Bryan could make an enemy, he would. I used to see the way he behaved with newspaper editors: if he met them the first thing he would tell them was what shits they were; but then he'd expect them to smile and say, 'Bryan, you're a genius—it's an honour to be insulted by the Laurence Sterne of his time'" (396).

The nearly tragic tale Coe has to tell of "Disintegration" (the title of his last section, taken from Johnson's 1964 novel, *Albert Angelo*) is followed, after the voices, by a Coda, called "Fragment 46," in which he poses the question "Why did B. S. Johnson cut holes in the pages of *Albert Angelo*?," tying the end of the book to its beginning, and records a series of enigmatic comments in Johnson's diaries about the White Goddess and a certain M who "wanted to go too deep" (38). Never claiming that he has discovered the key to the Johnson mystery or the figure in the carpet—although it seems very likely that he has—Coe has discovered a great deal about this M, a certain Michael Bannard, who was a friend of Johnson's youth, a character mentioned once under another name in *Albert Angelo*, a strange, flamboyant, sinister man who exercised some fascinating hold over Johnson. Bannard shared with Johnson an interest in "the Goddess," or the White Goddess, and had a strong objection to women; there is reason to think that the relationship between the two men was, or could have been if Johnson had not pulled back, a homosexual one. He learns that Johnson saw Bannard on the last night of his life, when his wife was away and he was desperate, and concludes that this "very complicated friendship, something much more fraught than the simple love affair between two men which I had been starting to construct in my mind" (434) explained very much about Johnson's life and death and, less certainly, explained the holes cut through pages of *Albert Angelo* as symbolizing the absence in that book of what Michael Bannard really meant. This explanation is offered tentatively, although it is built so powerfully that it persuades. The story reappears in altered but still recognizable form in *The Terrible Privacy of Maxwell Sim.*

Coe concludes the book with more personal revelations, including his own growing animosity toward Johnson during his eight years with the book: "Slowly, as I continued work on the book, this antagonism of Johnson's"—toward himself, he means, a hypothesized antagonism based on Coe's class position and more privileged life—"which I had intuited and which then wormed its way into my dreams—bred something similar on my side. My attitude towards him became more and more combative. Perhaps this needs to happen when you're writing biography" (452). His analysis of the relationship between biographer and subject is very subtle. Coe concludes with the declaration that Johnson's "novels challenge our most fundamental beliefs: our belief in the moral integrity of 'fiction'; our belief in the usefulness of storytelling when the daily truths thrown up by our misbegotten world cry out for immediate practical attention. The challenge is posed not just by his work as a whole, but by each novel individually" (454). As Johnson insisted on writing "novels" but rejected the idea of "fiction," Coe has written a work of nonfiction, which nevertheless brings to bear all the deepest and most original aspects of the novel.

FOUR

Breakthrough

When Coe's fourth novel, *What a Carve Up!*, was published, in 1994, it marked a major change in his career and in his fortunes in several ways. It followed a longer than usual spell between novels (*The Dwarves of Death* had appeared in 1990; his first three novels had appeared over just a four-year stretch). In the interval, Coe had written his two show-business biographies, on Humphrey Bogart and James Stewart, which he says were written almost entirely for money. The money served its purpose, helping to support him while he wrote the longer and much more ambitious book that came to be *What a Carve Up!*

His patience bore fruit in greatly increased visibility. *What a Carve Up!* won the 1994 John Llewellyn Rhys Award, given annually to the best work of literature, of any genre, written by a citizen of the British Commonwealth under thirty-five and published in English and in the United Kingdom In winning this prize, Coe joined such illustrious previous winners as V. S. Naipaul, Margaret Drabble, Jeanette Winterson, and Angela Carter. The following year the novel received the Prix du Meilleur Livre Étranger, a prize given each year by an informal jury of French literary directors to the best foreign book, putting him in the company of Gabriel Garcia Márquez, John Updike, and Mario Praz. Coe's celebrity in France is signaled by the prize; U.S. publication also followed in 1995, from Knopf, one of the most prestigious U.S. houses. Either because the film *What a Carve Up!* would be less well-known to American readers (in the United States it was released under the title *No Place Like Homicide*) or because (what amounts to the same reason) the phrase "a carve-up" is distinctly British, meaning something like "a dishonestly prearranged result," the American book was called *The Winshaw Legacy: or What a Carve Up!* There is a book within the book called *The Winshaw Legacy: A Family Chronicle,* so that title is promoted to the main title. The Italian translation, also published in 1995, was called *La Famiglia Winshaw,* while in France it appeared as *Testament à l'anglaise.*

Despite the six novels that Coe has published since 1994, for many observers *What a Carve Up!* is still his best work and he is, for them, "the author of *What a Carve Up*!" This cannot be wholly welcome, and he wrote in 2011 that "No middle-aged novelist who is still trying to make a living from writing likes to be told that his last five books are not a patch on the one he wrote when he was in his early 30s, but I suppose I'm obliged to entertain the idea that there might be something in it."[1] The note he strikes here is characteristically modest and balanced. Although he had published books before the one that became, for many, his signature accomplishment, there is still something here of the predicament of authors like Joseph Heller (*Catch-22*) and Alan Sillitoe (*Saturday Night and Sunday Morning*), condemned to go through a long publishing career known as the author of their first novels. Hence Coe's discomfiture; and yet he immediately acknowledges that the critics may be right.

Comparisons aside, there is no doubting that with this book he began to occupy a different position in British fiction, one in which it began to make sense to read that he is, in the words of his fellow writer Nick Hornby, "probably the best English novelist of his generation (my generation, as luck would have it)" or, as a critic wrote in a review of one of Coe's recent novel, "for the past two decades one of England's most admired novelists."[2] The shift from an author of two books he claims belong in the *Guinness Book of World Records* for poor sales, books he calls in retrospect "pinched and constrained," to an author with big sales, quickly issued paperback editions, reprints of those very same obscure early books, and U.S. and French and Italian publications must be attributed to the effect of *What a Carve Up!* more than to anything else. When the professor and newspaper columnist John Mullan chose a book by Coe for his Guardian Book Club, in 2011, he selected *What a Carve Up!* rather than any of the six books Coe has published since 1994.[3]

Finally, *What a Carve Up!* has attracted, by a comfortable margin, more academic criticism written about Coe than any other of his works. What is it in this book that marks a major change in his fiction? To oversimplify, perhaps, the book is distinguished by its subject matter, which gives it a much wider application and scope than anything in the first three novels; by its political stance, which, while not eschewing satirical and comic elements, is often one of outrage; and, most important, by its form.

Commenting in the *Guardian* in 2011, Coe himself makes some of the same points. He argues that "opening myself up to the idea of writing a socially panoramic story was incredibly liberating, and the fragmented, fast-changing nature of the reality I was trying to capture dictated that no single narrative approach would be adequate" (6). On the question of political commitment or anger, he expresses some doubts. In an earlier comment, he explained: "I began work on the novel in 1990, at the fag end of the Thatcher years, when I was 29 years old and flushed with political and literary certainties. The most fixed of these certainties was my anti-Thatcherism. . . . I wanted to express this pervasive sense of unease and betrayal, while somehow writing a novel that consisted of more than just liberal hand-wringing. One way of doing this, I thought, might be to try to tap into the energy and unpretentiousness of British popular culture—comedy in particular."[4]

As he readily acknowledges, there was nothing radical about a literary artist being anti-Thatcher; he estimates that 90 percent of British writers shared that stance of political enmity. It sometimes seems that Mrs. Thatcher, beyond anything else she may have done for or to her country, served the useful purpose of providing a productive hate-figure for novelists. So writing an anti-Thatcher novel would hardly distinguish Coe from many of his contemporaries: it is what he did with his anti-Thatcherism that counts.

The "present day" of *What a Carve Up!* occupies a fairly short period from autumn 1990 to January 1991, but the panoramic feature arises from its linkages backward through a whole range of British history from 1942 forward, although, it is true, most of the book concentrates on the Thatcher years, that is, from 1979 to 1990, and the Thatcherite policies that were continued in most respects under her successor, John Major, who is prime minister in the present-day sections. The novel is not about Margaret Thatcher as a person, and she is almost unmentioned by name; it is about the whole complex of attitudes embodied in the society that developed during her premiership, to some extent with her encouragement and that of her party. The ruling force was greed, and it was unleashed by a growing heartlessness about the weak and unfortunate. As Coe has explained, he knew he wanted to write about "Thatcherism," but he "wanted to express this pervasive sense of unease and betrayal"—felt by nearly everyone he knew—"while somehow writing a novel that consisted of more than just liberal hand-wringing."[5] Several decisions went toward this avoidance; in terms of subject and focus, the most important was to choose a single family, the Winshaws, as the representatives of the evils of the decade and to assign one of the Winshaws as the face of each of what he thought the most reprehensible evils. As Coe explains,"I sat down one morning beneath the benign dome of the British Library's old reading room . . . and drew up a list of six areas of public life I wanted to examine: finance, culture, politics, arms dealing, the media and food production. Each was to be assigned an individual member of my venal family, and then it was a question of delving into each area."

Each of these six representative Winshaws has an eponymous chapter: "Hilary" tells the story of one of the second-generation Winshaws who cynically enters into a journalistic career, ruthlessly betrays and sacrifices her mentor, and succeeds as a media commentator devoid of principle. The novel includes many of her contributions to public life, including two columns on Saddam Hussein, one of which praises him while the other damns him. There is her tabloidish feature "It's Boobs at Ten!," which is actually designed to distract readers from a High Court judgment against Mrs. Thatcher's government, and a column written in opposition to the striking coal miners' union that ends with "*How dare you put selfish greed before the national interest!*"[6] Coe's irony is deliberately hard to miss here: putting selfish greed before the national interest is the raison d'être of the Winshaw family.

Hilary's brother Roddy is an art dealer, who knows little about art but gives showings to the famous or well-connected or sexually appealing, regardless of talent. His most reprehensible action in the novel, aside from steadily driving down the nation's cultural level, is to pretend an interest in the paintings of Phoebe, an obscure artist from Yorkshire who works as a nurse. She spots the worthlessness of the work he usually shows, forthrightly calling it "Elementary stuff that wouldn't even have been given a pass at any decent art school . . . [paintings] which looked as though they'd been knocked off by some pampered socialite's daughter to pass the time between garden parties" (196). Promising that she will have her own show at his London gallery, Roddy seduces Phoebe in Winshaw Towers. The following morning he brutally offers her fifty pounds for one of her paintings, to cover a damp patch on a wall, and rejects the notion that her "student daubs" can ever appear in his Narcissus Gallery (212). In this he is assisted by his sister, Hilary, as they collaborate in corrupting the nation's cultural and intellectual life.

The other individual chapters are devoted to Dorothy, who has married an inoffensive farmer and turned his property into the nation's largest factory-farming business, with unimaginable cruelty to animals; Thomas, a banker and sex pervert; Henry, a politician who switches seamlessly from Labor to Conservative and plays a leading role in the Thatcher government; and Mark, an arms dealer. Here Coe comes closest to Thatcher, insofar as her son, also called Mark, was accused of involvement in the arms trade. Mark Winshaw encapsulates the unconcerned cruelty and the "putting selfish greed before the national interest" that are hallmarks of the family, as he enthusiastically markets weapons to both sides of armed conflicts. He cooperates with a German who is still a Nazi, leading to this conversation: the Nazi speaks: "'I know exactly what Saddam Hussein is making at his so-called research facility. I also know that Israel will be his first target. This is why I support him, of course. He will resume a process of cleansing which we were never allowed to complete. Do you take my meaning, Mr. Winshaw?' 'I make a habit,' said Mark, 'of not inquiring into the uses—'" (377).

Coe's suggestion of how the West turned against Hussein's Iraq (illustrated in Hilary's paired columns as well as the first Gulf War in 1991), appears in Mark's explanation to Henry (a politician who facilitates his activities, as Hilary provides journalistic support and Thomas supplies the money): "If it starts to look as though he's in a position to do any harm, then we find an excuse to attack him and wipe out the whole arsenal. And then we start selling again" (387). He urbanely reminds Henry, concerned about whether Saddam has the money to keep buying arms, that Kuwait is his rich neighbor; later the Iraqi invasion of Kuwait will become the "excuse to attack."

Thomas Winshaw illustrates many of the features of capitalism unfettered by principle or scruple; he invests in arms sales through Mark and he buys companies and depletes their pension funds, leaving retirees impoverished. He is particularly active in the Conservative "privatization" movement, that is, the sale of state services such as British Rail and British Airways to private investors. The narrator reveals that "He thoroughly enjoyed snatching these huge state-owned companies from the taxpayers' hands and carving them up among a minority of profit-hungry shareholders: the knowledge that he was helping to deny ownership to many and concentrate it in the hands of a few filled him with a deep and calming sense of rightness" (321).

One of Thomas's early investments is in the technology of video recorders. The explanation is that with the aid of a VCR he can pause films and gaze at actresses in *déshabille,* for masturbatory purposes, and the narrator suggests that "some people maintain that the phrase 'merchant banker' was introduced into the currency of rhyming slang"—meaning "wanker"—"at precisely this time" (309). Thomas's proclivities link him to the film *What a Carve Up!* since, as one of the studio's backers, he appears uninvited on the set for the filming of an important scene: the one in which Shirley Eaton, as the ingénue, takes off her clothes. Spotted peeping through holes in the wall of the set (these play an important part in the movie, in which they are also used for secret spying) he is frogmarched off the set by actor Sid James, despite his claim that he was only checking on the "soundness of the construction materials" (320).

This exact scene from the film has played a very important role in the early life of Michael Owen, the Winshaw biographer in the book, and will be duplicated later on in the plot. That Michael's father was the victim of Thomas's asset-stripping, leaving his retirement unfunded, and died of a heart attack caused in part by his eating the unhealthy food produced by Dorothy Winshaw's company is one of the many intricate connections in this novel.

Not all the Winshaws are monsters. The older generation also includes Mortimer, an ineffectual but kind man who inhabits Winshaw Towers, and Tabitha, who has been adjudged insane and confined to an asylum for decades. Their brother Godfrey, whose plane was shot down in 1942, was another of the good Winshaws, although his son Mark has turned out to be something of a sociopath (and is in fact working with the people responsible for the death of his father). Mortimer expresses his own judgment to Phoebe, whom he employs as his nurse after her encounter with Roddy: "'They're the meanest, greediest, cruelest bunch of back-stabbing penny-pinching bastards who ever crawled across the face of the earth. . . . There's only ever been two nice members of my family: Godfrey, my brother, who died in the war, and my sister Tabitha, who they've managed to shut up in a loony bin for the last half a century'" (209).

This account of the Winshaws demonstrates clearly what Coe meant by referring to his book as a panorama. What people eat; what they read; how they vote; where their money comes from; how their public services are funded or not funded (particularly the National Health, which, although not privatized, is "rationalized"—which in practice means demanding that hospitals and medical practices be operated like private industries and achieve "efficiencies" by cutting costs—and underfunded, with fatal results); when the nation goes to war and at whose behest; even what art is valued: all these are controlled, in Coe's synecdochic version of the Thatcher years, by Winshaws. This is a clever artistic choice, as depicting British society, in all its phases, over those years would be unbearably complicated, the result diffuse; for fictional purposes, Coe chose to assign six Winshaws to represent social reality.

Reviewers and critics seeking to characterize Coe's novel find a ready description within its pages, when Michael Owen, writing a book review, declares: "We stand badly in need of novels, after all, which show an understanding of the ideological hijack which has taken place so recently in this country, which can see its consequence in human terms and show that the appropriate response lies not merely in sorrow and anger but in mad, incredulous laughter" (277). It is typical of Coe's own mixture of laughter with savage indignation, as well as his comic handling of metafiction, that Owen concludes his review by declaring that the writer in question lacks the necessary brio for the task; as misprinted in a newspaper, where the problem becomes a lack of the necessary "biro" (a cheap ball-point pen), the complaint becomes meaningless, and the apparent declaration of an important critical and theoretical principle is reduced to bathos.

Many commentators on this novel have called it a condition-of-England novel. This term comes from the Victorian sage Thomas Carlyle, writing in "Chartism" in 1839, and has come to refer to novels—usually large or panoramic—that highlight important social questions. Victorian examples include Dickens's *Little Dorrit,* Trollope's *The Way We Live Now,* and Elizabeth Gaskell's *North and South;* more modern instances might be Margaret Drabble's *The Ice Age,* Martin Amis's *Money,* Zadie Smith's *White Teeth,* and Ali Smith's *Hotel World.* Coe is not entirely convinced, writing that "although it invariably gets described as a state-of-the-nation novel, I'm not even sure that *What a Carve Up!* fits that label. Readers wanting to get a handle on the glittering textures of the 1980s would be better off with Alan Hollinghurst's *The Line of Beauty;* those who want a chronological overview of the Thatcher years could try Tim Lott's *Rumours of a Hurricane.* My novel now [that is, 2009] feels to me more like the story of a depressed young hero going through a crisis of identity, while being swept along on a current of historical forces towards a destiny over which he has no control."[7]

The novel has two main strands—the panorama of the Winshaws and the society they illustrate and help to create and the personal story of Michael Owen, although these two strands are intricately and meaningfully connected at many points. Most critics, despite Coe's reservations, place the chief emphasis on the broad picture, that is, the state of the nation or condition-of-England portion of the book. Or, as Dominic Head has written, "there is an implicit debate about what kind of state-of-the-nation novel it is still possible to write."[8] Head claims that Coe's decisions prove his conviction that "an elaborate fictional form is required to offer a meaningful commentary on a fragmented society"; the versatility of its form he proceeds to characterize as "a work of high moral outrage that avoids polemics; a work of great flair that ranges assuredly between the poles of comedy and tragedy; a book that alludes confidently to both 'highbrow' and popular culture" (35). Anthony Quinn, reviewing the book on its publication, wrote that it "avows its political engagement with the sort of fury rarely witnessed on our weedy domestic scene."[9]

Terry Eagleton, whose political stance on the left probably makes him sympathetic to Coe's anti-Thatcherism, calls the novel "a social realist work, even if one of its most accomplished achievements is to press social realism just a hair's breadth this side of utter banality."[10] Ryan Trimm, a historian of Thatcherism and culture, expresses the same hesitation about Coe's realism, contrasting it with novels by Margaret Drabble, from which it differs, he maintains, because of the "predominance of a realist—or largely realist—vein in the other novels."[11] Richard Bradford defines it as "generally traditional and realist in form with a slight nod towards postmodernism," although this seems mistaken; if it is realist in intention, *What a Carve Up!* is certainly not traditional in form.[12]

Writing in 2003, Henry Sutton deplored the shortage of "gritty, politically engaged novels," insisting that perhaps "just two novels really stand out as having much of value to say about Britain in the 1980s and early 1990s, and where it was all going horribly wrong."[13] The other is Martin Amis's *Money. What a Carve Up!,* he writes, "was probably more overtly political in its wicked dissection of the Thatcher-inspired me, me, me generation and a group of toffs long past their sell-by date" (16). As is often the case, the author has shared his own thoughts on the political novel, mentioning the way the novel mocks Michael Owen, who is to some extent a fictional version of Coe (his two novels, *Accidents Will Happen* and *The Loving Touch,* are strangely reminiscent of *The Accidental Woman* and *A Touch of Love*). Coe explains, "I realized at that point that I had been taking myself far too seriously. As for addressing contemporary politics in a novel—well, that's always difficult, but no more so in Britain than in any other country, I wouldn't have thought."[14] He goes on to link this book with *The Closed Circle,* which also examines contemporary politics, acknowledging that for most people *What a Carve Up!* was more successful and offering reasons for this.

The state-of-the-nation novel traditionally includes analysis of class relations, and Coe's efforts in this regard have been judged inadequate by some observers. Nicola Allen recognizes Coe's effort to add a look at "the lives of the previously undocumented," mentioning the documenter (Michael Owen) but having little to say (as Coe, arguably, has little to say) about the truly marginalized, the poor and working class.[15] More forcefully, Dominic Head, in a contribution called "The Demise of Class Fiction," argues that the novel, even in the hands of "inheritors of the liberal-realist mode of political fiction, such as Martin Amis or Jonathan Coe, inevitably becomes a hegemonic tool, a reactionary cultural force that serves, broadly, to reinforce the status quo,"[16] and Lawrence Driscoll, along similar, roughly Marxist lines, points out that "Coe's own class position"—firmly middle class—"is elided while his work seems to have an almost magical power to take on Thatcherism and be able, single-handedly, to cut it down to size."[17] Driscoll believes that the novel itself inexorably speaks for the middle class; Michael Owen is middle class, no attention is paid to the suffering of working-class people, and hence "Coe's textual function is not to politically undermine Thatcherism from a socialist perspective, but to simply restore the culture to a middle class, decent, honorable center. This desire to attack Thatcherism for its greed, callousness, and its inhuman distaste for all things decent, leads Coe directly toward a satire of his social and economic moment, as opposed to any radical desire to overturn capitalism" (159).

Driscoll and Head criticize Coe from the left; a critic on the right, James Delingpole, reveals (in an interview with the author) that he wants to know "how an author of such evident skill and sensitivity could have written a book so bitter, so tub-thumpingly unsubtle, so glibly prepared to dismiss a whole class and political ideology as vile and worthless" as *What a Carve Up!*[18] He might well be nervous, as he had already reviewed the book as "quite the nastiest, crudest, chippiest, least generous book I have ever suffered the misfortune of reading a few pages of before giving up in disgust."[19]

Critics of Coe's political stance concentrate on his domestic, class-based analysis. But just as important is his uncompromising stance on British foreign policy, particularly its tendency to adventurist attacks in the Middle East under U.S. influence. In fact, three of his novels feature such a situation. In *A Touch of Love,* Robin is preoccupied with the American bombing raids on Libya in 1986, in which Margaret Thatcher's government made the British complicit by permitting U.S. bombers flying from British bases to make the assault. *What a Carve Up!* occupies the period running up to the first Gulf War, when the United

States and its allies, including the United Kingdom, moved from encouraging and enabling Saddam Hussein to war against Iraq in January 1991; *The Closed Circle* leads up to the second Gulf War, launched by President George W. Bush in March 2003. Coe's attitude toward all three of these events seems to be that the United States had insufficient warrant for its reckless resort to war, and the British had even less reason to align themselves with the Americans.

Unimpressed with Coe's class analysis, Lawrence Driscoll goes on for good measure to minimize the formal experimentalism of the novel, finally claiming that his break with conventional realism, since it leaves the class structure unsmashed, means that his "text is echoing and manifesting at a textual level what Thatcher's privatization of industry did at the economic level" (159). The meaning of this criticism is unclear; insofar as its premise is that the textual level of the novel should be aiming to undermine the state from a socialist perspective, it seems misguided as well. There are many observations to make about the technique of *What a Carve Up!,* and in fact this is, by most accounts, the most original feature of Coe's work.

Dominic Head explained the formal adventurousness as follows: "The state-of-the-nation novel, it seems, struggles to survive in its conventional phase. It now requires the rare ingenuity of a Jonathan Coe to breathe life into the corpse."[20] Among the most important products of that ingenuity are the parallel strands, or microcosmic and macrocosmic plots; the inventive use of film and, to a lesser extent, other popular culture; parody; and bricolage and intertextuality.

Such inventiveness has its detractors. British commentators often voice a suspicion of authorial cleverness (the phrase "too clever by half" does good service here), and the reviewer Hugh Barnes, for instance, in a mixed review, wondered why a gifted writer would rely on the cinema tradition of "Carry On culture" and concluded that the book "reads less like a study of the manners of a period than an inventory of the clichés of its entertainments"; another reviewer declared cleverness a mixed blessing, explaining that long novels are "already self-indulgent enough."[21]

Perhaps the key recognition is that *What a Carve Up!* is a mixture. It is not trying to achieve unity of tone or subject matter: quite the reverse. It is something like the book that Tabitha Winshaw (who, in the novel, has commissioned Michael Owen to write about her family) describes: "a tremendous book, an *unprecedented* book—part personal memoir, part social commentary, all stirred together into one lethal and devastating brew" (476). Most strikingly disparate are the two main plot lines: the story of Michael Owen and the story of the Winshaw family. Pamela Thurschwell comments on this, suggesting that Coe's novel "mirrors the double-structure of Dickens's *Bleak House,*" his 1849 novel, which alternates passages of present-tense, omniscient, panoramic narration with passages in which a young girl gives her own coming-of-age experience in the first person and in the past tense.[22]

The two strands in *Carve* are related, of course. Michael Owen is the designated chronicler of the Winshaw family, chosen (initially, it seems, at random after a chance encounter on a train, although readers learn later that the meeting was contrived and the choice planned) for that role. He meets the family; he is present at an art opening at Roddy's gallery and spends a weekend in a house where Phoebe (the artist mistreated by Roddy who becomes Mortimer's nurse) also lives. But the connections go much deeper. As Ryan Trimm comments: "Owen, though, cannot for the bulk of the novel, properly forge connections between the emotional privations of his own life and the carve-ups of Thatcherism and the Winshaws until he is able to grasp his own location in the tale. The key is an awareness of complicity. . . . Owen's epiphany [at the end, when he realizes he is central, not peripheral] is not the happiest realization, for it suggests a larger collision, one concerning his failure to stop the Winshaws and the values they signify" (176).

It is not entirely clear how Michael Owen could have stopped the Winshaws, who operate on a level almost inaccessible to him, but he is complicit in other ways (although most of his complicity is unknowing, involuntary, or both): participating in the final, fatal events at Winshaw Towers, discovering that his biological father was someone at the heart of the Winshaw's wartime activities, and even perishing in the crash of an airplane piloted by the deranged Tabitha. And if knowledge is complicity, his gathers speed when he learns how the Winshaws are partly responsible for the death of his (supposed) father and his friend Fiona. These connections are both dark and troubling and, as we would expect from Coe, sometimes playful and funny.

Lawrence Driscoll's dismissal of Coe's break with conventional realistic novel conventions serves as a useful reminder that much of the value of this novel centers in its formal qualities and that for most readers they are challenging, original, and successful.

The keynote of *What a Carve Up!* may be its inclusiveness. Already mentioned is its pairing of a panoramic condition-of-England story, rendered in tones of controlled fury, and a somewhat glum life story of an obscure writer, separate but not without linkages to the broad canvas. But this is just the beginning. The reviewer Hugh Barnes wrote that Coe "pulls in umpteen other stylistic and thematic elements: mystery-thriller, latter-day gothic, scathing ideological critique, brisk, expert political/social/economic analysis, love story, revenge tragedy and more"; Michiko Kakutani called the novel "part satire of Margaret Thatcher's England, part family farce and part detective story; a novel whose list of influences might include Moliere and Waugh and 'Beyond the Fringe'; a novel that simultaneously recalls Dickens's 'Bleak House,' the Alec Guinness movie

'Kind Hearts and Coronets' and Caryl Churchill's ferocious political satire 'Serious Money'"; Charles Gordon wrote that the novel has "elements of Lucky Jim, The Forsythe Saga, Ten Little Indians and the Bonfire of the Vanities, with some Ealing comedies thrown in for good measure."[23]

A French commentator, noting that *Carve* had "seduced the French to such an extent that it received the prize for the best foreign novel," praises its "subtle interaction between the public and the private, of constant comings and goings between the serious and the unusual, and of course, humour, but never too much of it."[24] She finds most striking "his fashion of anchoring his universal truths in the immediacy of contemporary society" (298).

The useful term for this kind of assemblage is "bricolage." This modern critical term, from a French word for tinkering or puttering around, means assembling an art work from diverse materials that happen to be at hand. Clearly "happen to be at hand" is not quite accurate when a creator selects diverse materials for a larger artistic or ethical purpose, but it gives the *effect* of Coe's work. There are two ways to see this in Coe's book. One is to recognize the relationships between his novel and various other texts (books by Molière, Dickens, Agatha Christie, a variety of films). This is *intertextuality:* the full range of relations among a text and its various predecessors (or intertexts), including quotation, allusion, and parody. Among the most important intertexts are three films: *What a Carve Up!* of course—seen, in part, by the young Michael Owen on his ninth birthday (a viewing aborted by his mother at the point when Shirley Eaton begins slipping out of her clothes—this is the scene Thomas Winshaw tried to peep at before being ejected by Sid James); *With Gagarin to the Stars,* a documentary about the Russian cosmonaut Yuri Gagarin, young Michael's hero (with whose life and death his story will be interwoven), which was showing on a double bill with *What a Carve Up!* on Michael's birthday; and Jean Cocteau's 1950 film *Orpheus.* These are not just touchstones, things characters remember (although Michael does remember and re-enact them); as Andrew Higson explains, in this novel "film features as subject matter, as structuring device, and as reference point or intertext."[25] Coe has always been interested in film, including demotic, lowbrow productions like *What a Carve Up!* and the more middle-brow works of Alfred Hitchcock or Billy Wilder (and, of course, Humphrey Bogart and Jimmy Stewart).[26] In the pairing of *What a Carve Up!* and *Orpheus,* he demonstrates the ready mixture of high and low culture that is a regular and agreeable feature of his fiction.

The film called *What a Carve Up!* was adapted from a 1940 novel by Frank King called *The Ghoul.* (King, despite his current obscurity, is a significant fixture in Coe's world, since his 1934 book *The House of Sleep* provided the title for Coe's next novel and appears in it as well). Chapter 1 of *The Ghoul* opens as follows: "The short November afternoon was fading into premature dusk. Thin, silent rain fell drearily. A dank, clinging fog had risen from the river, and was creeping furtively over the city. Through this grey pall the familiar roar of London's traffic penetrated, persistent, yet with an eerie muffled effect."[27] Chapter 1 of part two of *What a Carve Up!* begins with exactly these words except for the substitution of January for November (423).

Another way to think of Coe's bricolage is to acknowledge the heterogeneous types of material or texts contained within the pages of the novel. Terry Eagleton, in a strongly positive review in the *London Review of Books,* without using the term "bricolage," explained this second usage: "A carve-up of contemporary Britain, What a Carve Up! is also a carve-up of a book, a vertiginous, exquisitely calculated collage of texts-within-texts, of interviews, inventories and newspaper cuttings folded into a genealogy of the Winshaws which—since the narrator is struggling to write that genealogy—is also a record of his spiritual vicissitudes" (12). As Richard Bradford notes, the chapters on the Winshaw family "comprise a variety of discourses, including extracts from journals, newspaper articles, transcripts of radio and TV interviews, letters, all threaded along a rather dry third-person narrative. This is a patchwork of the basic material that Owen would draw upon in his account of the living Winshaws" (39), although the significance of this material goes beyond its being Michael's raw material. Most of it is not just satirical; it self-evidently condemns the Winshaws by means of their own words. Prime examples are the list of ingredients in one of Dorothy Winshaw's meal packets (255); the quotations from Hilary Winshaw's witless and yet sinister newspaper columns (72–77); and the printed transcript of a tape recording in which Mark Winshaw speaks coldly about weapons sales (389–390).

There is an art to making a collage, and the overall effect of Coe's use of this very wide range of different kinds of materials is carefully calculated and propulsive, rather than diffusive. Simon Dentith recognizes both the unity of Coe's narrative and his use of parody. Showing how two juxtaposed texts (a sentimental account of Hilary's marriage and maternity and a cruel conversation with a nanny in which she demands that "it"—her daughter—be removed for crying "is sufficient to discredit the parodied writing of Hello!"—that is, the cloying profile.[28] Dentith goes on to compare *What a Carve Up!* to Thackeray's novels, in that, like them, it "is full of the diverse languages of the contemporary world, many of them drawn from popular or commercial culture. This too is a novel which can confidently switch from a parodied and inauthentic language to one which reveals more accurately the contours of the world we actually inhabit" (74).

In addition to a fiercely penetrating critique of contemporary greed and immorality—and, it must be said, for some readers weakening it—is Coe's ever-present humor. He has said that he is "not interested in non-comic writing."[29]

There are grim smiles arising from the over-the-top hypocrisy of Hilary or the misanthropy of Dorothy or even the eccentricity of Tabitha. But there are more straightforward comic elements of language or event. The bathos of Michael Owen's review being ruined by the reversal of two letters, turning "brio" into "biro," is an example. A more developed example, and one thematically relevant since the novel critiques the Gulf War launched by the American president, follows: Michael, suddenly awakened,

> found himself staring at a face which would have struck terror into the heart of many a stronger man. Gaunt, misshapen and unhealthy, it expressed at once a meanness of spirit, a slowness of intelligence and, perhaps most chillingly of all, an absolute untrustworthiness. It was a face from which all marks of love, compassion, or any of those softer feelings without which no man's character can be called complete, had been viciously erased. It had, one might have thought, a touch of madness in it. It was a face which gave out a simple, dreadful message: abandon hope, all you who look upon this face. Give up every thought of redemption, every prospect of escape. Expect nothing from me.
>
> Shivering with disgust, Michael turned off the television, and President Bush disappeared from the screen. (423–424)

Laughter and sadness, popular and high culture, personal narrative and broad-canvas social diagnosis, Cocteau and Sid James: the mixture is accomplished, according to Eagleton, with "proper Post-Modernist irony" (12). The question of Coe and postmodernism occurs frequently, made more complicated by critics' inability to agree on what postmodernism is. So, for Richard Bradford, the book is "generally traditional and realist in form with a slight nod toward postmodernism" (40); by contrast, Anthony Quinn, reviewing the novel in the *Independent,* writes that with "a tricksy bit of postmodern footwork, the plot becomes a mirror of, and an analogue to, the denouement of the famous film" (26). The most thorough contribution to this question comes from Pamela Thurschwell, who refers to Coe's "postmodern pastiching" and declares that "Postmodernism's preference for comic forms can distract from the potential sadness of that dilemma"—that is, the author's inability to escape from the culture he critiques (29). She links the film *What a Carve Up!* to the Winshaws by recognizing its use as showing nostalgia for the *Carry On* style of films and their working-class humor, destroyed by the Winshaws' rapacity. Finally: "Throughout the book, Michael's dreams, desires and destiny are determined by the movies from *What a Carve Up!* to Cocteau's *Orphée,* to *With Gagarin to the Stars.* Like Woody Allen's essay in which his character gets trapped, first in *Madame Bovary* and then in a Spanish textbook, these narrative frames function in *What a Carve Up!* as unyielding fate (and also like that postmodern, strong-

Foucauldian version of hegemony in which juridical structures of power are totally determining and inescapable)" (33).

Terence Blacker, reviewing Coe's next novel, *The House of Sleep*, wrote, "For admirers of Jonathan Coe's acclaimed What A Carve Up!, this remarkable new novel will come as something of a surprise. Politics take a back seat, while satire and comedy are kept firmly on the leash, only to be released occasionally and to devastating effect. Compared with its flashy and overtly ideological predecessor, The House of Sleep is a creepier, subtler and more introverted novel."[30] This is an interesting assessment, in part because it inaugurates the critical practice of comparing Coe's novels to *What a Carve Up!* that will feature in his press again and again. Unlike Blacker, the reviewer Joel Yanofsky considered the novel to have "no shortage of comic set-pieces" and to be "loaded with put-ons, pranks and shtick."[31]

About satire, too, there is room for disagreement, as when Tom Lappin names Coe "a satirist whose eye for the ridiculous never seems to falter," while J. Bottum discounts Coe's satiric gifts (which he thinks are devoted to satirizing people's pretensions to need more sleep than others) because the story "just plods along." And Erica Wagner notes a changed focus for satire, which is embodied in Coe's "skillful plotting and sense of time-shift" devoted to "an inward journey through the subconscious."[32]

The most important features of *What a Carve Up!*—postmodernism; comedy; the mixture of styles, narrative strands, and types of discourse; political satire and criticism—carry over, even if mixed in different proportions, to *The House of Sleep*. Another link may be character: in a retrospective discussion of *What a Carve Up!* in 2011, Coe told John Mullan, "I wonder, though, whether the central character, Michael Owen, is really strong or sympathetic enough to support a lengthy narrative. He is a very passive figure, certainly. In fact, thinking about it, seven out of my nine novels feature or are narrated by passive, slightly depressed men—often failed writers or composers or both—who show a rather uncommitted sexuality and tend to fixate on past romantic disappointments."[33]

Although there are four main characters in *The House of Sleep*, arguably they are all failures of some sort—including a failed scientist, a failed film critic, and a failed secondary teacher; but the central character is Robert, who both fixates on past romantic disappointments and is decidedly uncommitted sexually. As Coe explains, "A man is in love with a gay woman and the only way he can win her is to become female. That was the premiss I began with. And it is what the novel is about, as far as I'm concerned."[34]

This is both useful and somewhat misleading, since, although it may be the book's origin and, to Coe, its subject, nevertheless large portions of the novel are not centered on Robert's love for Sarah.

Like *What a Carve Up!, The House of Sleep* is multifarious in many ways, including its subjects, its settings, and the nature of the documents it incorporates. As Peter O'Brien wrote, it is "part gothic horror story, part narrative of sexual awakening, part comic novel, part bildungsroman" and "a complex read that meanders back and forth through time."[35] Like *What a Carve Up!,* it is political, even if its political anger is less overt, targeting the ruthlessness associated with Thatcherism and the market "economies" introduced into many areas of public life; in this novel (as in the deadly results, for Michael's friend Fiona), the main locus of privatized public service is the National Health Service, with results both comic and catastrophic.

The paratexts prepare readers for this unusual reading experience. The table of contents shows that chapters are divided among sections named Awake, Stage One, Stage Two, Stage Three, Stage Four, and REM Sleep, followed by three appendices. The epigraph is from Rosamond Lehmann's *The Echoing Grove* (she is of course one of Coe's favorite authors, an object of his literary love affair, for whose reissued books, including *The Echoing Grove,* he wrote introductions); it consists of a quotation in which someone confesses to getting confused about time: "One gets outside the usual way of counting." There follows an Author's Note: "The odd-numbered chapters of this novel are set mainly in the years 1983–1984. The even-numbered chapters are set in the last two weeks of June, 1996."

The first chapter then plunges into the reflection by an unnamed man of a quarrel with a woman, resulting in the man shouting "BITCH!" in a public place.[36] This is an intriguing but intriguingly *misleading* start, as this shouter now disappears from the novel; the significance is that Sarah—who is a central character—mistakes the hurled insult as having been addressed to her and incorporates it into a collegiate discussion/argument about male privilege and feminism.

This occurs in the student hangout Café Valladon, which is one of the two locales important in the "campus novel" portion of this book. University students gather there and have the sorts of conversations university students regularly have. That is where Sarah meets Veronica, who later becomes her lesbian partner, on the day she is shaken by the shout of "Bitch!" Her recounting of this experience and Veronica's strongly feminist interpretation of the event as additional proof, if any were needed, that all men are misogynists and potential rapists creates the bond between them that will eventually become a love affair. As the café is one of the two nodes of the student life depicted in *Sleep,* the other is Ashdown, the house high on a hill outside town, where the students live. Scenes there revolve around Sarah's romantic life. As the novel opens, her boyfriend, Gregory, is demonstrating what a terrible person he is, playing games by pushing on her eyeballs and otherwise bullying her. When she tells him she is not in the mood for sex, he responds, "But we've had the foreplay and everything" (15). They break up, and Robert, new in the house, becomes interested in Sarah, but before anything can come of this, she falls in love with Veronica and they begin living together. Robert remains rather pitifully her friend.

The 1980s material is similar to plot elements generally found in novels about university students: they sit and drink coffee and talk; they make and break and remake sexual connections; they experiment with gender; they argue about politics and literary theory; they think nervously about life after graduation. All this occurs, in pieces, in the alternating chapters set in the 1980s. In the contemporary chapters—set in 1996, the year before the book was published—the aftereffects appear. Gregory is now a sleep therapist, and Ashdown is his residential clinic for the treatment of various sleep disorders. One of his patients, Terry Worth, was a student at the university and a friend of Robert's, although not a resident of Ashdown. Again, the facts come out gradually and fitfully, and there is a greater focus on Gregory, on Terry (a patient who used to sleep all the time and now never sleeps), and nurse Cleo Madison. Sarah's life is now in London, where she is a primary school teacher.

The two temporal sections of the novel are linked in several important ways. The obvious one is that the 1990s chapters reveal the later lives of the students. As Ben Platt commented, "Coe creates an interplay between his characters' younger and older selves. The beauty of the novel emerges in the shifts of time and in the way these failed, fractured people rediscover and, often unwittingly, help one another. . . . Ultimately, these fragile chains of human interaction add up to an unexpectedly unified whole, in a style that recalls the fiction of Virginia Woolf."[37] Platt's view was not unanimously endorsed, of course; for instance, Suzanne Berne complained that toward the end the book almost turned into a house of cards as its "mazy style is abandoned for a sudden rush to connect all the stray paths that have been meandering through the novel."[38] Careful readers will find that the characters and plot lines are also linked thematically, particularly through issues of sleep, including sleeplessness, cataplexy, narcolepsy, plaguing dreams, and (in Sarah's case, most crucially) inability to distinguish between dream and waking reality. They are also linked by setting. As Coe has explained, in a comment on his website explaining the book's origin, he thought of the book as being made of two stories: one was about a man "so deeply in love with a gay woman that he is prepared to do anything to win her affection"; the other was about patients in a sleep clinic. Finally he realized that location could be the link, and Ashdown—student residence in the 1980s, sleep clinic in the 1990s—was the result.[39] Linguistically the chapters are linked as well, through a device that may seem a gimmick. Chapter 3 ends in the middle of a sentence, with "Robert realized that he had trusted Sarah with secrets about himself, about his parents, about his home life, that he had never thought" (56); chapter 4 begins (in the 1996 range) with "thought there was something strange about the rooms at the Dudden Clinic" (59).

One example of these important linkages also demonstrates the author's very careful management of his intricacies. The walls of Café Valladon are lined with books. Terry shows Robert, at one point, that he keeps a ten-pound note secreted in the shelved copy of *Great Expectations,* for future needs. Veronica and Sarah like to read a book called *The House of Sleep;* and Robert tells Sarah that if he ever leaves anything for her he will leave it on page 173 of that book. Time passes. In 1996 Sarah meets a woman, the mother of one of her pupils, and, looking around her book collection, sees *The House of Sleep.* She is of course struck by what seems an unusual coincidence, since this is a rare book. This discovery leads to another: this woman was the partner of Veronica, who had abandoned Sarah on graduation; opening what she thinks is a second copy of *The House of Sleep,* implausible as that seems, there Sarah finds a poem, written by Robert and left there for her. This complicatedly advances the plot toward its somewhat open but nevertheless apparently "happy" conclusion.

The ending of chapter 17 shows that *Great Expectations* was also carefully chosen to be the hiding-place book; it reads, "The evening mists were rising now, and in all the broad expanse of light they showed, Cleo saw no shadow of another meeting with her" (311)—an intertextual invocation of Dickens's revised ending, in which Pip says of Estella, following almost exactly the same lines about mists and light, "I saw no shadow of another parting from her."[40] Pip has been hopelessly in love with Estella for a long time, as Robert has with Sarah, and has tried to make himself over to win her—to make himself a gentleman. Robert more drastically has made himself a woman.

As an intertext, the book *The House of Sleep* is carefully chosen for its role in Coe's novel: a pop-culture text which Sarah and Veronica enjoy in a camp way—"entranced by its dated 1930s jargon and the incredibly convoluted plot . . . a baffling series of midnight kidnappings and grisly assassinations" (118)—it provides a powerful reference to Ashdown, both as student residence where students sleep and Sarah suffers sleep disorders and as the Dudden sleep clinic. Finally, *The House of Sleep,* a real book, was written by Frank King, who was also the author of *The Ghoul,* filmed as *What a Carve Up*!, the intertext, or one of them, for Coe's previous book.

The bricolage effect of that book is carried forward in *The House of Sleep.* There is a master narrative, fairly traditional in impact even if not in chronology, delivered by a third-person narrator with ready access to multiple characters' minds (Coe's standard narrative approach). Within this there are many other types of discourse: by page 9, in the final evening of Sarah and Gregory's relationship, there is a transcript of analysis, with lines attributed to "analyst" and "analysand." It is immediately evident that the analysand is Sarah; the analyst is introduced much later, in the "present-day" chapters, and further pieces of the transcript appear further on. There is a film review, written by Terry Worth, which ends with flippant irony; Sarah, reading the review but missing the irony, gets into trouble as a result: she takes a sad pupil to see the film, thinking it is a different sort entirely. But this "trouble"—a stern denunciation by the pupil's mother—produces enlightenment, as this mother is the one whose copy of *The House of Sleep* contains Robert's poem, and she is able to tell Sarah about Veronica's fate (a fatal car crash).

There is a rap, written by one of Sarah's secondary pupils, and a poem, written to Sarah by Robert. Several more documents, beyond his review of *Chalk and Cheese,* concern Terry in his roles of film critic, cinema historian, and admirer of obscure movies; one is an entry in an encyclopedia about a missing Italian film that obsesses him (one frame from the movie bizarrely connects with Robert and Sarah's story). The novel's appendices consist of Robert's poem, a letter from Terry's mother, and a transcript of a somniloquy, that is, what a character says while asleep (or in this case while pretending to be asleep). The richest heterogeneous document is a short article called "Fragments from a Life in Movies." A tedious and uninteresting memoir written by an old filmmaker and edited by Terry, it is disfigured when Sarah, at Terry's request, removes one of the footnotes but (sleepily) fails to remove the number, thus making each succeeding number off by one. The comic results include, for instance, a footnote after an account of Pope Paul VI's praise of some inspiring works: "Their titles, for the record, were *Wet Knickers, Pussy Talk* and *Cream on My Face*" (271) and a footnote identifying Cliff Richard (a perennial pop star in the United Kingdom) as "one of the undisputed queens of British popular music" (274). The reaction to Terry's article puts the journal out of business.

This episode is the clearest example of Coe's continuing insistence on comedy in what is, by most measures, a very somber novel. Another impressive passage, in Stage Four, brings together a group of doctors for a mandatory workshop organized by "Hengleton Pendlebury . . . one of the country's most prestigious firms of management consultants" (251). (The practice of entrusting hospitals and the nation's health care to "managers" rather than doctors is an ongoing scandal highlighted by Coe.) The episode is important in many ways. It provides a pulpit for Russell Watts, a ridiculous Lacanian psychotherapist who has treated Sarah (the earlier transcripts are from his analysis) who, in reading his case notes, humiliates Gregory (another attendee) because of his principled refusal to change patients' names. But Watts is satirized in his own way, mostly because of his strenuous linguistic Freudianization of Sarah's case (the case is entitled "The Case of Sarah T.: or, an Eye for an 'I.'" (283). At one point he tells the other impatient physicians: "Language is a traitor, a double agent who slips across borders without warning in the dead of night. It is a heavy snowfall in a foreign country, which hides the shapes and contours of reality beneath a cloak of nebulous whiteness. It is a crippled dog, never quite able to perform the tricks we ask of it. It is a ginger biscuit, dunked for too long in the tea of our expectations, crumbling and dissolving into nothingness. It is a lost continent" (282–283).

Not satisfied, he later goes on to say that language is "a sly cardsharp," "a distant flute on a misty night," "a fork in the road; it is a knife in the water" (293). His blinding preconceptions lead him to conclude that Sarah suffers from a desire for the phallus and that her eyes represent "two vaginas which some freak of nature had placed on either side of her nose" (293). They prevent him from recognizing Sarah's narcolepsy, which is obvious to another, more sensible doctor present.

The conference is worthless, and Coe has some fun indicating how: the facilitators write pointlessly on a flip chart; they require participants to engage in "creativity enhancement procedures" (253); they put on silly hats. All these stunts are proudly proclaimed to be taken from American management consultants, and these doctors have been required to attend by the "managers" of their new hospital trusts. Here Coe is (as in the hospital events of *What a Carve Up!*) pointing out the folly of the Thatcherite efforts to rationalize the provision of medical care, to make it a market operation like any other (hence the hospital "trusts"), to subordinate medical options to market decisions.

As Professor Cole—who effortlessly recognizes what was wrong with Sarah from Watts's account—complains, "It seems to me entirely appropriate that I should end my career making collages out of paper and glue, under the supervision of a man ten years younger than my younger son" (257). For him, and not just for him, the conference is worse than a waste of time, because he should have been attending a meeting to decide on how to treat a dangerous schizophrenic; his "trust managers" are of course arguing for his release, since that improves the profitability of the trust and thus the manager's performance in crude "bottom-line" terms. While Cole plays a game called "Alien Babies" in a hotel, elsewhere the dangerous schizophrenic is released; soon he encounters Terry Worth on an underground platform and knifes him, leaving him in a permanent coma.

The anti-Thatcherite critique of the marketization of health is paralleled by the identification of the rather monstrous Gregory Duddon as an admirer of Mrs. Thatcher. Her chief appeal to him seems to be her ability to go without much sleep, as he has bizarrely concluded that sleep is itself a disorder, something human beings can be trained to do without. If it is an impressive accomplishment for Margaret Thatcher to sleep only two or three hours a night, then how much more impressive to go without sleep entirely. His training, mostly applied to animals but on at least one occasion to a student subject, with fatal results, consists of cruelly behaviorist efforts to eliminate sleep. As the novel closes he finds himself wired up to a machine, moving on a turntable, presumably to his death, to the sound of Pavarotti's "Nessun dorma"—none shall sleep.

As is usual, Coe manages to insert political and psychological depth and seriousness into a narrative that is also rich in metafictional technique (or perhaps the infiltration goes in the other direction). *The House of Sleep* is, the reviewer Michael Wood wrote, "so intricate, so dependent on surprise and on characters showing up in altered circumstances" that it was hard to review without spoiling the plot.[41] David Nokes praised the novel for its jokes, but more because "The House of Sleep is also a House of Games. Coe is an enthusiastic deviser of postmodernist puzzles, constantly embellishing his text with parodies of Lacanian psycho-babble, spoof literary allusions and a film-buffs bluffer's guide. The whole novel, with its careful scattering of clues and codes, is a semiologist's wonderland, full of false trails and elusive signs."[42]

Anti-Thatcherism, playfulness, mixture of the serious and the comic, experimentation with form—all these are familiar in Jonathan Coe's oeuvre. What is new is the prominent interest in the fluidity of sexual identity. We recall that he identified the prompt for the novel as a man in love with a gay woman who can win her only by becoming a woman. This makes it sound simpler than it is in the book; for one thing, the first time Robert, now a woman, arranges to meet Sarah at Ashdown, she speaks to Sarah before disclosure and hears Sarah mention *her* plan to marry a man and runs humiliated from the house. Sarah reflects back on this encounter (later in time although earlier in the pages of the novel), thinking, "Twelve years had gone by, twelve years since she had last seen him (she could not count their last farcical encounter at Ashdown, even though that in its way had been the most bruising of all)" (105).

The narrative leaves some ambiguity on how radical Robert's change is—that is, if it is utterly against his own deep inclinations, and thus a very great sacrifice, or whether he might have been inclined, if only slightly, in that direction already. After all, the first night Sarah meets Robert, a new inhabitant of Ashdown, she barges into the bathroom to find him in the tub and shaving his legs, an act that to him has "some fundamental quality of rightness" (50). Later, while Sarah is living with Veronica, Robert objects to urinating standing up—the idea "repulsed him" (227). Most strongly, on a memorable occasion when Robert and Sarah go to the beach (along with Ruby, a neighbor child who plays a crucial role in bringing about the resolution of the novel through information provided in her "somniloquy"), the narrator reveals Robert's feelings about his own penis: "How he loathed and despised this preposterous organ, with its infinitely predictable patters of behavior, its changeless, robotic responses to an over-familiar range of visual stimuli" (153). (That his erection comes in response to glimpses of Sarah changing into her bathing suit is another clear indication that Robert's sexual interests are in women, despite his somewhat indecisive commitment to traditionally male gender characteristics or, perhaps, attraction to some characteristics gendered female.) Henna Venho also notes, in addition to his dissatisfaction with his own sex, "his envy of female privileges," instancing Sarah's capacity for self-deprecation.[43]

The important connection between sleep disorders and Robert's sex change comes from the fact that Sarah, whose narcolepsy includes imagining things that have not happened, becomes mistakenly but strongly convinced that Robert has a twin sister, Cleo. She tells him that he would be perfect "if it wasn't for . . . a certain something"—presumably his "preposterous organ"—and goes on with "it should really be me who goes off looking for Cleo. Just imagine it—your twin sister: a female you. That would be my ideal partner, wouldn't it?" (241). So Robert *becomes* Cleo. In the failed first meeting, he insists, "You said it"—her ideal partner—"would be a female me. My twin sister. That's what you said," but at this point Sarah is entering a heterosexual marriage (310).

That Robert becomes Dr. Cleo Madison; that she works for Gregory Dudden in the sleep clinic; that she encounters Ruby and Ruby notices a scar on her ankle, the result of Robert/Cleo having cut herself when Sarah entered the bathroom unexpectedly, and remembers seeing that scar on Robert at the beach; that Ruby brings about a reunion between Sarah and Cleo once she realizes who she is; that Ruby does this by making herself a patient and pretending to be asleep, delivering a "somniloquy" that includes Sarah's address in London; that she does this because, on the beach, Sarah told her "nobody would ever tell a lie in their sleep" (164): all this is part of the incredibly detailed interweaving Coe manages in this book. Another step toward Sarah and Robert's reunion comes when she discovers, in the pages of *The House of Sleep* on the shelf at Veronica's former partner's house, the poem he had written for her during that same day at the beach (it appears as an appendix, under the title "Somniloquy"). This poem is a rich node of connections. In it, Robert uses the phrase "your narcoleptic eyes"; this brilliant stroke of diagnosis is comically undermined, however, by the reader's having earlier seen Robert in the throes of composing the poem, trying out other modifiers, chosen because they fit the meter, including "blue remembered eyes," "multicoloured," "polymorphous," "diatonic," and even "antiseptic" eyes before settling on the only one that is actually true and related to sleep. The poem also reveals that Sarah's disregard had "made me feel unmanned" and goes on to "pray for an oblivion so deep / It ends in transformation" (Appendix 1)—all this before sexual transition has become a possibility. In most senses, Robert's transformation has not only been foreshadowed; it appears as a positive development. Venho notes that it shows his "resourcefulness and strength of character" and suggests that "a greater wisdom may be discerned beneath the actions that are originally ostensibly motivated by his sheer, unwavering aspiration to 'earn' Sarah."

It is here, too, that Coe brings in Simone Weil again; on the beach Robert is reading *Gravity and Grace,* her posthumously published book alluded to in *A Touch of Love,* and his poem begins by testifying "Your gravity, your grace have turned a time / In me, no lunar power can reverse" (Appendix 1).

Robert's change, Sarah's coincidental discovery of *The House of Sleep* ("this house of sleep" is another phrase from Robert's poem, by the way), and Ruby's mediation are linked, as well, to a dream of Terry's—one in which he envisions a woman dressed as a nurse standing in front of a sign saying "fermer." He connects it to his interest in Italian cinema and thinks the sign may say "infermeria," but, since Cleo is a nurse and Sarah lives on Fermer Road, it is one more link that strengthens the "happy ending"—not an explicit one, but happy enough in that it places Cleo at Sarah's door, and Cleo thinking "she had been lying to herself; knew that she could not do without this woman at all. It wasn't possible, and never had been" (331). The convoluted events that must occur to bring Cleo to that door—overheard conversations, remembered shaving scars, falsified somniloquies, a copy of Frank King's *The House of Sleep* that turns up, in Jonathan Coe's *The House of Sleep,* where it is completely unexpected, and a man's sacrifice of his sexual identity for the woman he loves—constitute an extraordinary exercise of fictional skills.

The successor to *The House of Sleep, The Rotter's Club,* resembles it in its political engagement, although the politics are those of the 1970s rather than the 1990s (or the 1980s as featured in *What a Carve Up!*); it is closer to *Carve* in being something of a condition-of-England novel; and it delivers male protagonists who, like Robert in *The House of Sleep* and Michael in *What a Carve Up!,* long for love but are ineffectual in obtaining it.

FIVE

The Trotter Stories

Beginning with the publication of *The Rotters' Club,* in 2001, Coe turned to a different project: a series. It ended up being a series of two, but the two were very tightly connected, sharing a cast of characters, a narrative explanation, similar themes, and plot points that were raised in one book only to be settled in another. How did this come about? Coe has provided an explanation: "In the back of my mind I wanted to write six volumes . . . and when I started writing The Closed Circle that's what I did, only that I skipped volumes two, three, four, and five."[1] Elsewhere he has explained the gap: "'I like the idea of a big caesura between the narratives, a space which readers can fill in with their own speculative history,' he says. 'It's a kind of dyptych, or a trilogy in two volumes, or a roman fleuve with bits missing."[2] He also (he has said) planned to publish the two volumes six months apart, but "BS Johnson got in the way."[3] The reference of course is to the biography of B. S. Johnson, *Like a Fiery Elephant,* which was planned to take two years but instead occupied about seven, so there was a caesura in the author's life as well as those of his characters.

Jenny Turner most fully explains the effect of the relationship between the two books:

> Coe has said that when he began "The Rotters' Club," the plan had been to construct a six-volume saga of Birmingham life, a Midlands version of Anthony Powell's "Dance to the Music of Time." Then he changed his mind. Wouldn't it be more interesting just to write the first volume and the last one, leaving everything in the middle a big blank? Such opposite impulses—to grand sweep and attenuation, earnestness and jokiness, realism and antirealism—are what lend Coe's fiction its rhythm, its pleasures and its frustrations. . . . The symmetries developed between this novel [*The Closed Circle*] and its predecessor appear more intricate and abstract the

> longer you reflect on them, and yet, around these axes, much of the novel has a free-form, improvised quality.[4]

Having read *The Closed Circle,* however, one will not find "everything in the middle a big blank"; through authorial provision, reported conversations, and other means, including a straightforward synopsis printed at the end of *The Closed Circle,* the reader is well informed about what has happened in these characters' lives in the two-decade-long caesura. There are no books about the 1980s or 1990s, but the later novel undertakes to cover many of the developments of those decades—an obligation that may contribute to what some readers see as its less satisfactory coherence. As for the idea of a roman-fleuve, associated with Proust and Balzac, Richard Eder suggests that it is "a river indeed, though page by page it is more of a heartbeat thumping between a systole of comedy and a diastole of anger."[5]

The Rotters' Club shows some evident connections with its two predecessors, *What a Carve Up!* and *The House of Sleep.* One suggested continuity is that it continues Coe's anatomy of modern British society by decades, or at least by perceptible eras. As Florence Noiville commented, "After publishing *What a Carve Up!,* a ferocious comedy of the Thatcher years . . . Coe, with *The Rotters' Club,* offers a deep plunge into the 1970s: the years of Edward Heath and James Callaghan, of punks and Genesis, marches against the Common Market and strikes at British Leyland."[6] Although *The Rotters' Club* is not about the entire 1970s, covering only the six years between 1973 and 1979, it ends on the night of the day when Margaret Thatcher was elected prime minister, so it does slot neatly into the anti-Thatcher focus of *What a Carve Up!;* it is, as Chris Lehmann wrote, a "beautifully composed novel of Britain on the brink of Thatcherdom."[7] Reviewers, perhaps primed to see Coe as a condition-of-England specialist, regularly made the same observation as Noiville: Simon Edge, for instance, wrote that the "novelist who made his name with his savage Eighties satire *What a Carve Up!* has now turned his attention to the previous decade."[8] Coe has considerable play with features of the decade that, although perhaps colored by his own nostalgia (for the 1970s were the years of his own secondary education, so that his characters are his own contemporaries), also stand out in retrospect as embarrassing: brown wallpaper, certain excesses in popular music, and hairstyles. William Sutcliffe's review elected to link the new novel to its predecessors in other, less chronological ways: "The comedy and brio of *What a Carve Up!* is here in force, yet that book's rather broad-brushed approach has gone, replaced by the more personal, intimate voice of the far darker *The House of Sleep.* With this novel, Coe seems to have taken the best aspects of both books, and fused them to lift himself on to a new plane of achievement."[9]

Like *The House of Sleep, The Rotters' Club* has a distributed focus, featuring four or five central school friends, the girls they are interested in, and many of their parents: a large cast altogether. It is true that Ben Trotter is regularly read as the main character, perhaps because the novel's title comes from a schoolboy joke in which he and his sister, Lois Trotter, are nicknamed Bent Rotter and Lowest Rotter and in part because he seems to be something of an autobiographical figure, something close to the author as a teenager. As Coe has explained, Ben is based on the young Coe, although "I'd rather have been Doug, the politically clued-up one who wangles a job writing for the NME and is good at getting laid. He's a sort of fantasy alter-ego."[10]

Though in a different way from *What a Carve Up!,* this novel combines a personal narrative and a political one. It is both a coming-of-age novel about adolescents making some sort of adjustment to the world and a broad-canvas account of the changes, particularly the more unsettling ones, that confronted the United Kingdom between 1973 and 1979. These include IRA bombing, labor strife and strikes, and racial hatred and upheaval. While Ben Trotter and his schoolmates are concerned, like many boys their age, primarily with school trends, friendships, love, and sex, they are implicated in the larger events of Coe's story; as Pamela Thurschwell puts it, "Coe punishes his intensely exasperating but likeable protagonists by making them unable to escape defining events of their childhood (events they use to escape the socio-political world they are exhorted by others to more fully inhabit). Benjamin Trotter in *The Rotters' Club* experiences his own family's brush with tragic history when his sister Lois's boyfriend Malcolm is killed in the Birmingham IRA pub bombings in 1974, and Lois herself is traumatized for years. He also lives tangentially through the labour struggles accompanying the crumbling of union power in the 1970s."[11]

Aside from the features already mentioned—a broad social and political canvas of Britain in the 1970s, an intimate and personal narrative of boys and girls reaching toward adulthood, and important linkages between the two—it is not just an interesting biographical fact but an important critical point that *The Rotters' Club* was, from the beginning, planned to be the start of a series. Despite being called a *roman-fleuve* and linked to Anthony Powell's *A Dance to the Music of Time,* this seems excessive (Powell's series comprises twelve novels); nevertheless, it is a series. As John Mullan notes, "a narrative might refer proleptically to what will occur beyond its own ending."[12] A famous example is Dostoevsky's *Crime and Punishment,* which includes on its last page (in the Constance Garnett translation), "He did not know that the new life would not be given him for nothing, that he would have to pay dearly for it, that it would cost him great striving, great suffering."[13] Coe's, unusually, ends with an "Author's Note" announcing, "There will be a sequel to *The Rotters' Club,* entitled *The Closed Circle,* resuming the story in the late 1990s."[14] As Mullan comments, "Many novels have sequels, of course, but it is unusual for the first work to point forward to an as yet non-existent follow-up" (185).

Creating the two novels as a unit required that he plan very carefully: Mullan notes that he "inserted into *The Rotters' Club* hints as to what would happen to them"—his young characters—"in a later fictional life" (186). Among these are some fairly heavy dramatic ironies; for instance, on the last page, Sam Chase (father of one of Benjamin's schoolmates) makes two predictions, as cheerfully reported by Ben Trotter: "Number One, you and Cicely will have a long and happy life together, and of course I laughed at that, because I know that it's true, and then he pointed at the newspaper someone had left on the next table, it was a copy of *The Sun,* with a big picture of Mrs. Thatcher on the front page, Number Two, he said, that woman will never be Prime Minister of this country, and then we both roared with laughter and clinked our glasses" (399).

Readers will know how far off the mark Sam was about Mrs. Thatcher, in this novel about "Britain on the brink of Thatcherdom,"[15] and will discover in *The Closed Circle* that he was equally wrong about Ben and Cicely. Coe confirmed to Vanessa Guignery that the two books "were heavily pre-planned and the conclusions of the books were already in my head when I started to write them. In fact with those books I started with the endings and then worked towards them."[16] With his usual lack of arrogance, his willingness to assess his own work objectively, Coe goes on to suggest that this may have been harmful to *The Closed Circle.*

In a sense, *The Closed Circle* is present from the beginning of *The Rotters' Club,* since the earlier novel starts in 2003 with two young people, Sophie and Patrick, sitting down to dinner in Berlin. They are the offspring of two of the characters seen as adolescents in *The Rotters' Club* and, having met accidentally, begin to talk about their parents' young lives and eventually begin to tell each other the story. Sophie explains, "Come with me, then, Patrick. Let's go backwards. Backwards in time, all the way back to the beginning. Back to a country that neither of us would recognize, probably. Britain, 1973" (3); she continues with some easy contrasts that show how different Britain was thirty years earlier—without PlayStations, Princess Diana, or Tony Blair, but with unions powerful enough to shut down power stations and deny the nation electricity.

Since *The Closed Circle* covers the years between 1999 and 2003 and was published in 2004, Sophie and Patrick are in effect looking back from the world of that novel. It is not quite clear, however, what the purpose of this overture is or why Coe has elected, or affected, to assign the narration of the story to Sophie, with all the privileges of knowing people's secret thoughts and terrors, reading the school newspaper and sampling Benjamin Trotter's private writings: in fact, despite occasional insertions such as "I'm doing my best, Patrick. Really I am. But it's not an easy story to tell, the story of my family" (10), the remainder of the novel does not particularly feel as if it is being narrated by Sophie. The aim of the beginning may be to assign to a second-generation character the "placing" of the 1970s, although the tone is slightly mawkish and at the same time "knowing," with an insider's knowledge, and so not very convincing coming from a person who is equally unfamiliar with life before PlayStation and Princess Diana and who can have learned about the 1970s only secondhand.

At any rate, the narrative proper begins on the next page, on November 15, 1973, and in the family home of the Trotters. The domestic scene provides important exposition, social location for the Trotter family, and character insight into the individuals. Mrs. Trotter is reading the *Daily Mail,* a middlebrow tabloid paper. The furnishings, including a coal-effect fire, establish the middle-classness of the Trotters. Benjamin Trotter is doing his homework (he will prove to be the most serious student). Lois Trotter is reading *Sounds,* a weekly magazine about popular music, specifically the personal ads, looking for a boyfriend. And their younger brother Paul, "precociously, is reading *Watership Down: "Simple African villagers, who have never left their remote homes, may not be particularly surprised by their first sight of an aeroplane: it is outside their comprehension*" (9). Paul's precocity will be much in evidence in both novels; *Watership Down,* published in 1972, is a temporal note, and the racism of the passage prepares readers for Paul's own racial attitudes, displayed as the novel proceeds.

The most important development of this early scene is that Lois finds a notice that seems meant for her: "Hairy Guy seeks Chick. Birmingham area" (13). The Hairy Guy will prove to be Malcolm, with whom Lois falls in love and who is killed by an IRA bomb in the Tavern in the Town as Malcolm is on the point of proposing marriage, to the tune of "I Get a Kick Out of You," when the bomb goes off.

Other strands of the narrative are launched in these early chapters. Ben and Lois Trotter's father, Colin, meets with other managers and representatives of the unionized workforce at Longbridge, the British Leyland car manufacturing plant where he works. Although the talk is of an end to the class war, the novel features much labor strife, a strike at Longbridge, and the decline of British manufacturing. One of the other men at the meeting, Bill Anderton, provides additional linkages in the narrative fabric of Coe's novel: his son Douglas is one of Ben's friends and one of the central schoolboys in the plot; Bill Anderton himself has an affair with Miriam Newman, a typist at Longbridge, whose mysterious disappearance remains unsolved in this novel, while Miriam's younger sister Claire is a contemporary of Ben's whose interest in him goes unappeased because of his unshakeable attraction to the lovely, fascinating, and maddening Cicely. The narrative moves back and forth between school and homes, between schoolboys and (to a lesser extent) girls and their families.

There is ample variety of tone. The affair between Bill Anderton and Miriam Newman is serious, involving Miriam's demand that Bill leave his wife for her, a blackmailing note from another union steward who threatens to inform Irene Anderton of her husband's infidelity, Miriam's disappearance, and even a dubious (but apparently true) claim by Paul Trotter that he had seen her naked by a reservoir before her disappearance.

A comic counterpoint is supplied by the "affair" between Mr. Plumb, the art teacher, and Barbara Chase, mother of Ben's friend Philip; it begins on a parent-teacher night at the school, when Plumb astonishes her with his cosmopolitanism, which contrasts comically with her own naiveté, as when he asks her, "You don't know *The Virgin and Child*?" and she replies, "We don't get out to pubs much" (50). The full blast of his vocabulary includes the declaration that Barbara's likeness to a painting is "quite thaumaturgic" and the observation that schoolboy Sam's imagination is "both antic and phantasmagoric" (50). The epistolary affair continues ("*Only when we are together, coalescent, infibulate, will I attain that fugitive condition of* nirvana *which has been the sole* desideratum *of my infructuous, miscarried existence*" [142]), excitingly although sexlessly, with Barbara unable to break it off and her husband, Sam, a bus driver who feels unable to compete with such erudition and savoir-faire, responding by self-education and vocabulary building. By the end of the book, he is reading *Ulysses.*

School stories tend to return to a few common situations or memes. The central character is usually a sensitive youth, not particularly athletic but cleverer than most; he may well write or compose or edit a literary magazine; all these details apply to Ben Trotter, and in them he resembles schoolboy protagonists from Stephen Dedalus in *A Portrait of the Artist as a Young Man* (1916) to Christopher Lloyd in Julian Barnes's *Metroland* (1980). He has begun a comic novel, "not yet daring to admit to anyone, even his closest friend, that he had undertaken this ambitious project, or that in doing so he believed he might have found a vocation, an area of creative obsession which seemed likely to rival or even to overtake his tentative musical activities" (57). These musical activities, by the way, consist of listening to lesser-known groups like Hatfield and the North (whose song "The Rotter's Club" provides the title), playing keyboards in a band called Gandalf's Pikestaff, and composing tunes like "Apotheosis of the Necromancer," which is described by a bemused friend, looking back, as "a rock symphony in five movements, totaling some thirty-two minutes in length (i.e. even longer than 'Supper's Ready' from the Genesis album *Foxtrot*), and narrating the entire history of the universe from the moment of creation up until roughly, as far as I could make out, the resignation of Harold Wilson in 1976" (179). All his artistic endeavors are subjected to an irony, gentle enough to reveal that he is not untalented, just juvenile. He is too shy to speak to girls.

The most crucial event of his school years explains his religious devoutness. Having forgotten his swimming suit on a day of swimming lessons and aware that school policy requires a person in that situation to swim naked in front of all the other boys, he utters a silent prayer to God to provide a suit, finds one on a nearby bench in the changing room, and turns to Christianity.

He has a small circle of good friends and a somewhat larger circle of friends who are not so close, among whom the most important, thematically, is Richards, the only black pupil in the school. Even those who like him call him Rastus, thoughtlessly, unaware of its offensiveness. Richards is one of the outstanding boys in the school: the best athlete, a fine actor, the boy Claire Newman identifies as "the one boy in your year that *everybody*'s crazy about" (93). Richards is opposed by and victimized by the boy identified as "their old enemy Culpepper: junior rugger captain, junior cricket captain, would-be athletics champion and long-standing object of derision" (25). Despite this derision, Culpepper is genuinely insidious; he is openly and positively racist about Richards, both from conviction and from envy of Richards's successes (including breaking Culpepper's arm on the rugby pitch). In the end he seems to drug Richards to make sure that he performs badly on his exams and is refused admission to the university of his choice.

Richards just keeps on being victimized: near the end of the novel Ben, working in a bank while waiting for university to begin, denies a loan to a small fish-and-chip shop seeking to expand and later learns sickeningly that the Richards family had pinned its hopes on the business.

Another more ambiguous pupil is Sean Harding, "the class jester, the school clown" (174). His talent is for going too far, for instance, completely blacking his face with ink for a discussion of *To Kill a Mockingbird.* On another occasion he somehow plants a pair of his underpants so that a particularly sweaty teacher will use them publicly as a handkerchief. He writes letters to the school newspaper, signed as Arthur Pusey-Hamilton, MBE, imitating the kind of letters often written to right-wing papers by retired right-wing colonels (using language such as "Gladys, my good lady wife") and expressing frightening reactionary opinions on such matters as interracial kissing and the desirability of arming school prefects with truncheons. But no one is quite sure what Harding actually believes, so the irony remains uneasy.

The school story is, of course, linked to events in the larger world. Douglas Anderton's father, a senior shop steward at the British Leyland plant, is involved in the labor struggles of the 1970s, which indeed persuaded many voters that Mrs. Thatcher was the solution to Britain's problems. Richards's struggles against ingrained racism are a microcosmic version of the nation's macrocosmic struggles to accommodate a multiracial society and workforce. In the auto plant a group called The Association of British People circulates a pamphlet declaring that "Neither Heath nor Wilson nor Thorpe [that is, the leaders of the Conservative, Labor, and Liberal parties] has the will to stop the tide of coloured immigration into this country. All are slaves to the liberal establishment way of thinking" (38). It goes on to a numbered series of claims about black men's inferiority. Its language is reminiscent of Culpepper's when he tells the boys that their English master, Fletcher, is "a dreadful old liberal softie. He wouldn't let anyone get away with impersonating a nigger" (25).

During a 1976 meeting of the Debating Society, Harding, in one of his ambiguous jokes, speaks on behalf of the National Front candidate, receiving six votes. But "the NF candidate in the actual by-election did much better" (178). The National Front, a neofascist nativist organization founded in the 1960s, grew much stronger in the 1970s; it demanded an end to all nonwhite immigration and the repatriation of previously admitted nonwhite immigrants, as well as the return of capital punishment. It reached its peak of success probably in 1976. The Association of British People, responsible for racist leafleting at Longbridge, would be in sympathy.

Other key social issues that form the larger superstructure of which life at King William's School is the substructure include a nascent women's liberation movement, felt here mostly as the dissatisfaction and restlessness of traditional housewives (a good example of which is Ben's mother's decision to take a job outside her home) and anti-Irish feeling, also manifested at the auto plant and partly explained by the IRA campaign to "bring the war home" to England—that is, to import some of the ongoing violence of the Northern Irish "troubles" to the home country, in terrorist incidents designed to turn the English public against government policy in Ulster. Bombs exploded in pubs, in London's Post Office Tower, and outside the Old Bailey law courts and in department stores during Christmas shopping. The deadliest incident was the Birmingham pub bombings of November 1974, which killed 21 people, including Malcolm the Hairy Guy, and injured 182, including Lois Trotter.

The effectiveness of terrorist bombing comes from its apparent randomness and its targeting of civilians; Lois and Malcolm's involvement cannot be called an accident, since the bombing was an intentional act, but *it is an accident for them.* They have chosen their venue because a friend told Malcolm not to go to The Grapevine, which would be full of "cunts in suits" (100).

Coe explores the dark ironic possibilities of the bombing by having it follow closely on Malcolm and Lois's having told each other of their love, talking of how happy they are, and sharing an unspoken proposal: "Of course she knew. And of course, Malcolm knew what her answer would be. They understood each other perfectly, at that moment. They were as close to each other, and as close to happiness, as it is possible for two people to be. So Malcolm never did ask the question. Then, at 8:20 precisely, the timing device set off the trigger, the battery pack sent power running through the cables, and thirty pounds of gelignite exploded on the far side of the pub. And that was how it all ended, for the chick and the hairy guy" (104).

Lois takes a long time to recover from her trauma, understandably since the novel reveals later on that she was left holding Malcolm's head in her arms.

All these developments—IRA threats, racial disharmony, labor troubles, even musical revolutions—are part of history, but they are incorporated by Coe as part of personal history. *The Rotters' Club* does not feel quite like a "historical novel," in part because the historical events are introduced with some delicacy and always linked to plot developments. The musical revolution is a good example: Benjamin's band, Gandalf's Pikestaff, actually has only one rehearsal; *while it is going on,* the drummer and guitarist rebel, turning Ben's rock symphony into a punk-rock thrash, the lead singer screaming out the words (taken from Harding's National Front speech the previous day) "The maws! The maws! The very maws of doom!" (180)—a phrase that becomes the new name of the school's new punk band. Microcosmically, punk has displaced pretentious electronica; where *Tales of Topographic Oceans* was is now "Never Mind the Bollocks." Earlier Ben's little brother Paul—identified as precocious—has been repetitiously singing, "I am an anti-CHRIST / I am an anar-CHIST" (211)—lyrics from the Sex Pistols' *Anarchy in the UK,* released in November 1976.

Changes in musical fashion may seem relatively unimportant compared to deadly bombings and racist political parties, but in Coe's work at least they are not. Music is never casual. His own history as a musician finds traces in all his fiction, perhaps most strongly in *The Dwarves of Death* and the short fiction *9th and 13th;* he still thinks of himself as a composer, as he told Francois Gallix and Vanessa Guignery, with "novelist" his third-choice career and film director second (36); he listens to music while writing and is deeply knowledgeable about all kinds of music. But, beyond his own passion for music, it plays an important narrative role in his work. Explaining its use in *The Rotters' Club* (and *The Closed Circle*), he said, "I use music differently in those books because when looking back at 1970s and my own childhood . . . one of the things I remembered is how important pop music was to anyone growing up in Britain in the 1970s and to what extent people, particularly young people, defined themselves by what kind of music they listened to, and how it said everything about you, about your intellectual pretensions, about your political views, all these sorts of things. Someone who would listen to Bob Marley was very different to someone listening to David Bowie, who was very different to someone listening to Van der Graaff Generator. So the musical references in those books are actually very much part of the characterization" (37).

Claus-Ulrich Viol remarks, concerning Paul's singing the Sex Pistols song, that it "is highly emblematic of the book's construction of the 1970s as a 'golden age' that is brought to its downfall by the sinister forces of dynamism and movement." While Paul is always shown as "disruptive, spiteful and evil, he in this passage additionally stands for speed/movement and noise."[17]

It should be clear that politics are important in *The Rotters' Club,* including both broader, national politics—the rise of the National Front, for instance, and local labor strife that becomes nationally inflamed—and local politics, of the sort parodied by Sean Harding or embodied by the conflict between Richards and Culpepper or the controversy over the semisecret Closed Circle group. Readers will expect, correctly, that Coe's position is on the left. As Chris Lehmann sums up, "Coe remains an acidic and unapologetic partisan of Old Labour and its various long-neglected affiliate causes" (T07). The contemptuous phrase "dreadful old liberal softie," used by Culpepper to dismiss his English master, probably applies accurately to many of the positions embodied in this novel. It is clearly opposed to racial hatred, white supremacist politics, and race-based anti-immigrant policies. It exposes the evils of the creeping merchandising of all aspects of modern life: the best example here is the commercial sponsorship (by Ladbroke's, the bookmaker) of the traditional Oxford-versus-Cambridge boat race. Microcosmically, the Closed Circle group calls for reform of the school, along what would soon be recognized as Thatcherite lines, insisting that King William's School must "MODERNIZE"—including putting it on a fee-paying basis rather than accepting government subsidy—"RATIONALIZE"—by reducing the number of pupils—and "AGGRANDIZE"—by publicity designed to overcome the disadvantage of a Birmingham location (287). The Closed Circle itself is an ideal engine for this change (according to Paul Trotter) because it enjoys secrecy and unaccountability, patronage from sympathetic masters, and elitism: it "does not have to listen to the voice of the rabble . . . it is anti-democratic, and that is its strength" (287–288). That the Closed Circle is a metonymy for the coming Thatcherite/Blairite changes in British politics of course becomes more evident in the next novel.

Coe presents as disastrous the poor performance of British manufacturing and the resulting loss of jobs and whole industries and the vitiation of the labor movement. Bill Anderton, union man, is dispirited by the meeting at which British Leyland's new chairman persuades the union to vote (715 to 5) in favor of his proposals, which include the loss of 12,500 jobs. Anderton, a flawed but sympathetic figure, reflects that "there had been plenty of days, good days, and not so long ago, when he truly believed that the struggle could be won; but the decade was old now and he was growing old with it, and he knew that those days would never come back" (304).

Alluded to rather than directly narrated is one more important historical movement. Benjamin refers to "Doug's article this week, Doug's article for the *NME*"—*New Music Express*—"about Blair Peach and what happened in Southall"

(365). The event he alludes to combined electoral politics, antiracist activism, organized labor, and increasingly unaccountable government. Reading of it in the *NME* even links it to the musical revolution of the 1970s. Peach was the president of the East London Teacher's Association and a member of the Socialist Workers' Party; he was also an antiracist campaigner, who on the day he was killed, in April 1979, was leading a demonstration against the National Front in Southall, East London. He was knocked unconscious and died the next day; most of the evidence, including a delayed inquest (made public only in 2010), showed that he had been killed by a Metropolitan policeman.[18] Although this event belongs in the late-1970s milieu, it has been criticized: Stephen Amidon, writing in the *Atlantic Monthly,* declared that his "evocation of police brutality against striking factory workers reads like plain old agitprop, and his inclusion of the IRA's horrific Birmingham pub bombings in the narrative is awkward and ultimately bathetic."[19] Of course, readers differ widely on how welcome they find overt, even committed, treatment of political matters in their fiction. Paul Gilroy, in an essay focused on Britain's "postcolonial melancholia," declines to explore the novel's "mixture of *Bildungsroman,* thriller and comedy," choosing instead "to focus on that perennially unfashionable dimension: its loud and unusual antiracist advocacy. In doing so, I do not want to give the impression that this is a didactic book. It is not, even though racism is situated at its core, telling us something profound about the character and the boundaries of English national consciousness."[20]

Coe has described his novel as panoramic, and, reaching as it does into so many lives and touching on so many events and ideologies, it cannot have the tight economy or formal unity of an Anita Brookner novel or, for that matter, *An Accidental Woman.* One unifying feature is the unsettling figure of Paul Trotter. This precocious boy is never fully at one with his family; as Ben reminds Lois (recovering from her trauma), "*We're* the Rotters' Club. You and me. Not Paul. Just you and me" (171). Paul is unsentimental, unfamilial, illiberal. Although the younger brother, he seems older, as when he tells Ben, "Now that my weak-minded brother has fallen into the hands of religious maniacs, I have to keep a protective eye on him" (92). He even has the sexual confidence that Ben lacks, confidently addressing older girls with impertinent remarks. There is little suggestion that he is actually interested in the opposite sex, although he enjoys having seen a naked girl earlier than his older brother.

It is in his operations at school that his malignity most shows. He aligns himself with Culpepper and is admitted to the Closed Circle. This is described by the narrator (Sophie?) as "a select debating society, composed of no more than sixteen members at any one time, drawn mostly from the upper sixth and very occasionally from the year below"—so that Paul's admission, from a lower year, is also precocious—and by Doug Anderton as "a nasty, divisive bit of elitist bollocks" (145); intruding into their conversation (on the bus home from school), Paul insists that "Elitism's a good thing. Everyone but a handful of blinkered ideologues knows that. Elitism leads to competition and competition leads to excellence" and plans to request admission (146). In a letter to the editor of the school paper, Culpepper (alongside nativist slurs on Richards) reveals the sequel:

> The sixteen members of The Closed Circle, a "think-tank" composed of the finest minds in King William's (to which Mr. Richards has not, I believe, been elected) last week held a fascinating discussion on the subject of "continuity and change." A most telling point was made, on this occasion, by the newest of our members, P. D. Trotter, who has recently secured election at the unprecedentedly young ago of thirteen. Trotter made the observation that only people with a deep love and knowledge of tradition understand it well enough to realize that radical, sometimes brutal measures can be needed to keep it alive. Modernize—modernize or die, was his rallying-call: a slogan that should be pondered long and hard by Mr. Richards and all those like him—including the members of the present government—whose complacent, backward-looking attitude has led this country into its present state of social and economic inertia. (228)

The fullest explanation of Paul comes in a speech given by Douglas Anderton in 1999, the text of which is printed proleptically in *The Rotters' Club.* It is about Bonfire Night (Guy Fawkes Night), November 5, in 1976. Douglas introduces Paul Trotter, although not by name (by 1999 he has become highly visible in the Tony Blair government): "There was something strange, something freakish about this boy. He was wise—or at least intelligent—way beyond his years. He was a Midwich Cuckoo, and he scared the shit out of us" (181). Paul comes running up to Doug, with a sparkler in his hand: "At that precise moment," Douglas recalls, "his sparkler fizzed out. I didn't say anything, so he supplied the answer himself. 'The death of the socialist dream,' he said" (182). Anderton's speech goes on to mention those "Quixotic" things his father and others had dreamed of—a national health service, redistribution of wealth for a fairer society, and equality of opportunity—and acknowledges that they will not happen. The passage ends with "Goodbye to all that" (182).

This short list of noble aims, seen in what registers as a long, sad farewell, qualifies as a good enumeration of the positive political values of *The Rotters' Club,* one may say. Generally the novel seems to uphold the desirability of the goals of postwar Labor politics; more accurately, it implicitly endorses anything that Culpepper and Paul Trotter deride. One positive, although perhaps sentimental, positive value is community, and it is embodied in a memory Benjamin has of Christmas night, 1977. He sits in his family home with his parents, his beloved grandfather, his cat, and Lois; they are watching the *Morecambe and Wise Christmas Show* (a very popular comedy feature on BBC Television). This was the last such show to be on BBC, the state-owned network, as the two famous comedians moved to Thames Television, a commercial channel, the following year, a development reminiscent of the commercial sponsorship of the Oxford Cambridge boat race.

> Suddenly, sitting entranced before the television, Benjamin had a fleeting vision: it came to him that he was only one person, and his family was only one family, out of millions of people and millions of families throughout the country, all sitting in front of their television sets [viewership was 28 million, about half the United Kingdom population], all watching these two comedians, in Birmingham and Manchester and Liverpool and Bristol and Durham and Portsmouth and Newcastle and Glasgow and Brighton and Sheffield and Cardiff and Stirling and Oxford and Carlisle and everywhere else, all of them laughing, all of them laughing at the same joke, and he felt an incredible sense of . . . oneness, that was the only word he could think of, a sense that the entire nation was being briefly, fugitively drawn together in the divine act of laughter. (274)

This vision is qualified by the fact that Lois, still traumatized, is not laughing and Paul is not even with the rest of the family: he is upstairs, reading a book by Milton Friedman, economic guru to the Reagan and Thatcher revolutions. Ben's vision does lead to an idea of vocation, deciding that, beyond his ambitions as a writer or composer, "to be a bringer of laughter was in fact the holiest, most sacred of callings," but soon the vision is shattered and "once again everything in his life seemed fraught, complex and uncertain" (274–275).

As Coe has insisted, "every new book that you write requires a rethink," so readers will not expect that *The Rotters' Club* will be written in the same way as its predecessors.[21] Arguably it is less innovative than *The House of Sleep* or *What a Carve Up!* There is a fairly clear chronological line that runs from beginning to ending, varied by occasional flashbacks and retrospects and even a flashforward, Douglas Anderton's speech, that is from the material of *The Closed Circle;* there are multiple characters, and their multiple consciousnesses are shared with the reader, but these characters all stand in comprehensible relations to one another. The three techniques that stand out are the narrative framing, the use of multiple documents in a bricolage technique, and the final sentence.

It has been mentioned that the novel begins with a short introductory excerpt set in 2003, in which Sophie and Patrick (who are the daughter of Lois Trotter, Benjamin's sister, and the son of Philip Chase, Benjamin's best friend) begin to tell each other stories of their parents. This frame is partially closed in this book and appears again toward the end of the next one, *The Closed Circle.* The "partial closing" may be explained by Patrick's words, "stories never end, do they? Not really. All you can do is choose a moment to end on. One out of many" (402). The meeting between these old Birmingham friends and their children years on in Berlin (with a sensational swoon by Lois as the band plays "I Get a Kick Out of You," the song that was playing when the fatal bomb exploded) provides exposition neatly. But it is hard to understand how Sophie and Patrick could have come to know what Benjamin felt on Christmas night, or how he exulted after sleeping with Cicely, or what Bill Anderton said to Miriam Newman, and this narrative choice has provoked some controversy: Ian Sansom, for instance, insists that "the framing device for his new novel . . . seems to be held together with two blobs of mastic, intended to provide a solid fixing onto a sequel," and Adam Mars-Jones becomes more specific: "it's an oddly self-defeating device. If Coe acknowledges the help of a dozen or so books for his reconstruction of a period he remembers (born 1961, he is a contemporary of his adolescent characters), it's hardly possible that young Sophie, a child of the Thatcher years, could improvise the whole thing with such command of detail, minutiae, for instance, of prog-rock bands thrown out of fashion like so many genteel Rattigans by the Angry Young Men of punk. Her stylized hesitations last only a page or two, and after that it's hard to remember the point of view from which this narrative is supposed to emerge."[22] Such "problems" are not decisive or destructive, finally, and the return to 2003 helps to close the narrative, or close the circle, in the second book.

Coe had been working with diverse written and printed materials in his novels for some time, and in *The Rotters' Club* these include quite a few issues of "The Billboard," the school newspaper for which Benjamin writes and to which Harding sends his spoof letters; excerpts from inflammatory pamphlets; letters, including those from Mr. Plumb to Philip's mother and one from Emily Sandys to Claire Newman telling the story of Lois and Malcolm; and selections from Lois's diary. These detail a family camping trip to north Wales during which Benjamin reunited with Cicely. There is a transcript of a taped interview Claire Newman conducted with Bill Anderton for "The Billboard": although the main subject is labor trouble at Longbridge, Claire succeeds in getting Anderton to talk about his affair with Miriam and his conviction that she is dead.

The most important interpolated document is the most thoroughly explained: "On Monday, 13th December, 1999, Douglas Anderton, along with five other figures from public life, took part in an event called 'Goodbye to All That' at the Queen Elizabeth Hall in London" (174). This was an end-of-the-millennium event. The printed version of Anderton's speech includes his accounts of Harding's National Front address; the single rehearsal of Benjamin and Philip's Gandalf's Pikestaff, which turns into a punk performance; and the events of Bonfire

Night, with Paul Trotter giggling over "the death of the socialist dream." Another longer interpolation consists of Benjamin's account of a holiday in Denmark where his family confronted anti-Semitism and Paul saved another boy from drowning. This is explained as a story found in Benjamin's papers, a longer version of one that won him a prize for creative writing at school. John Mullan links this "inset narrative" to Fielding, in whose work Benjamin is reading obsessively during the Danish vacation; he goes on to explain its function—not so much in this novel but in *The Closed Circle,* where the boy whose life Paul saved reappears as a manager for the BMW firm that takes over the Longbridge plant—and as "a kind of descant" that "tells you of the fear and loathing that youth incubates," although he considers its provenance—the explanation of how it comes to be in the book—awkward.[23]

The technical innovation that attracted most journalistic attention was the final sentence of the novel, which runs unbroken from page 363 to page 399 of the hardback and is about fourteen thousand words long. Coe commented that he did it as an experiment and to change the tone; he continued, "I was aware James Joyce had done something similar but that is more fragmented and impressionistic. People who would not read *Ulysses* have not found a problem with it. I didn't set out to beat any records but it might be the only one I get, so who knows I might have a go at it."[24] The inclusion in this long concluding sentence of Sam Chase reading *Ulysses* is probably not an accident: more likely it is an *hommage* to a predecessor's long concluding sentence. It tells how Benjamin finally slept with Cicely, how confident he was that they would be together forever, how hilarious it was that they did it in Paul's bedroom on the day when Margaret Thatcher, unexpected by them, would be elected to lead the country. He is ecstatic, but the novel is constructed to show how wrong he is, how little the readers should trust his claim that "we have all been too sad for too long, and nothing is going to go wrong ever again, not for me or for Cicely or for Lois or for anybody, it's all a joke, everything is a big wonderful joke" (398). Pamela Thurschwell comments that Benjamin's "is the wrong kind of laughter. A willful disregard for the political sphere will never lead to happiness in Coe's universe" (37). The form and length of this sentence are, finally, less sensational than reviewers seem to have believed; more important is the way it ends: "it seemed to me then that not only does God exist but he must be a genius, a comic genius, to have made everything in the world so funny, everything from Sam and his crazy predictions right down to the dark beery circle my glass has just left on this green coaster" (399). Readers of *Ulysses* will remember that its final sentence, Molly Bloom's soliloquy, ends with "I asked him with my eyes to ask again yes and then he asked me would I yes to say yes my mountain flower and first I put my arms around him yes and drew him down to me so he could feel my breasts all perfume yes and his heart was going like mad and yes I said yes

I will Yes."[25] Both are powerful affirmations; Coe's, however, is undermined not only by the reader's knowledge that Sam was wrong about Thatcher but by the evidence plentifully supplied in the sequel.

The Rotters' Club was made into a three-part television series that was screened on BBC in 2005. It was well received by reviewers and viewers.[26] The broadcast led to some new appraisals of the novel, including Carola Long's declaration that "*The Rotters' Club* has become, for those of a certain generation, the defining novel of Britain in the 1970s the way that *The Bonfire of the Vanities* defined America in the 1980s."[27] Coe has written about how pleased he was that the adaptation was written by the celebrated scriptwriters Dick Clement and Ian La Frenais, whom he considered heroes, especially for their show "Whatever Happened to the Likely Lads?," which was first broadcast in 1973 and 1974. He continues: "In my most formative years, in my teens, I wasn't reading novels at all, I was watching telly, and what I was watching most of all were Whatever Happened to the Likely Lads? and Porridge. . . . I've always thought that nobody writes better serio-comic dialogue than Dick and Ian."[28] It may be too much to claim that the television program "inspired" the novel, but it was a part of the popular culture out of which Coe's novels have grown, as much as they have sprouted from Henry Fielding and B. S. Johnson.

As promised at the end of *The Rotters' Club* in 2001, *The Closed Circle* followed in 2004. It begins with a series of letters, addressed to "Sister Dearest," written from Etretat, France, in December, 1999; they are unsigned and for a time some mystery persists about who is writing to whom. Readers are primed to expect a holdover character from *The Rotters' Club,* and references to Philip, Benjamin, and Doug Anderton confirm those expectations. Gradually details emerge that show that the letters were written by Claire Newman to her sister, Miriam, who disappeared in the earlier novel; that Claire has been married to Philip Chase and is now divorced from him, although amicably, and has a son named Patrick; that Benjamin is married to Emily, without any children; that he is supposed to be writing a grand masterpiece but nothing has come of it; that Benjamin still (or again) plays in a band and, when the band plays "Seascape No. 4" (written for Cicely), that he has never gotten over her, although clearly his expectations at the end of *The Rotters' Club* of their eternal union have come to nothing. Near the end of this short series of letters, which very artfully provide considerable needed exposition, Claire writes, "I'm glad that I went to hear Benjamin play tonight. Do you know why? Because I learned in a priceless instant that he is still lost, still in thrall to the past, and I saw the pain that he's causing because of it, and I realized that I cannot possibly live my own life that way. I'm not talking about Stefano [her Italian ex-lover], I'm talking—regrettably, my much-loved sister—about you."[29] In other words, after years of telling herself that her sister was still alive and might receive messages, she "must start by doing the hardest thing of all—the thing I've been resisting all this time—and give up hope" (34).

Claire's letter makes several neatly woven connections with the predecessor novel. In one of them Claire writes to Miriam, "already I'm faced with a blast from the past. It comes in the form of a flyer I picked up at the Queen Elizabeth Hall. There's going to be a reading there on Monday, the title of which is 'Goodbye to All That'. Six 'figures from public life' (it says here) are going to tell us 'what they most regret leaving behind or what they are happiest to see the back of, at the end of the second Christian Millennium'. And look who's number four on the list: no, not Benjamin (although he was the one we all thought would be a famous writer), but Doug Anderton—who we are told is a 'journalist and political commentator', if you please" (7).

Douglas Anderton's contribution to this event has been one of the most revealing documents, particularly about Benjamin's band and his brother's character, in *The Rotters' Club.* Claire goes on to express her surprise that, when she is alone with her son Patrick, despite his introversion, "when he *did* start talking, the subject he chose was the last thing I'd been expecting. He started talking about you, Miriam. He started asking questions about when I'd last seen you, and how Mum and Dad had coped with it when you disappeared" (13). Readers will recall that Patrick is one of the two members of the next generation (Sophie, Benjamin's niece, being the other), and his interest in his mother's stories of the past may help to explain how his knowledge about his parents and their friends provides the frame for *The Rotters' Club.*

It is tempting to take as the novel's motto Claire's resolution to give up hope, although that may exaggerate the despair Coe displays. Most of the characters shown earlier as schoolboys and girls have failed to satisfy their promise or achieve their ambitions: Benjamin, more clearly than anyone else, has fallen short of the accomplishments he aspired to and, as Claire reveals, his friends expected for him. Benjamin's future is part of a series of "fulfillments" this novel supplies for its predecessors.

Some of them show the outcome of plot developments or the weaving in of loose ends from *The Rotters' Club.* For instance, readers learn, through the persistence and intelligence of Claire Newman, what happened to her sister, Miriam. More thoroughly, and ironically, the sequel to Benjamin's happy promise of a future with Cicely at the end of *The Rotters' Club* is explored. She left him the next day, as it happened, moved to the United States, and began a lesbian phase. He married Emily but, as his friends can tell, has never gotten over Cicely, and toward the end of *The Closed Circle* she returns and they are reunited. It is hardly the dream future he imagined, as Cicely has lived a hard life, with multiple partners, and by the time she returns to Birmingham she is ill: on her first reappearance, although unidentified, she turns up at Benjamin's flat, leaning on a stick, and "Her face was bloated and sickly, and the woman's figure was stout, but there was about her, at the same time something formidable and imperious" (340). At the end of the novel, Philip reports that she and Benjamin are together and that, even though on his visit she "was sitting there in her wheelchair, ordering him around like a fucking dog," (379), Benjamin is happy.

On a much less eventful level, the apparent miracle of Benjamin's swimming suit is explained. In *The Rotters' Club* he is saved from having to swim naked, after forgetting his bathing suit, by the unexplained appearance in the locker room of a spare suit. In *The Closed Circle* this is traced to the gamy proclivities of a visiting homosexual poet. Since Benjamin had accepted the suit as resulting from divine providence and had become a Christian on the strength of this "miraculous" answered prayer, finding out where it really came from cancels his faith.

One of the most sinister characters in *Rotter* is Paul Trotter; in *Circle* his future is portrayed: he is a member of Parliament, a minor adornment to the Tony Blair administration, whose utter lack of principle, mistreatment of his family, and tergiversation on whether the nation should go to war in Iraq are synecdoches of the Blair administration itself, portrayed here almost entirely as a disappointment to the hopes of the voters and a betrayal of the real values of the Labor Party. As Doug Anderton explains, "most of them"—the voting public—"still believe that they've voted in a left-wing party. Whereas really they've just voted for another five years of Thatcherism" (130). There is a funny scene between Anderton and Paul Trotter in which Douglas tries to get Trotter to reveal his "core beliefs" and to define the "third way"—an empty slogan used by the Blair administration and one Paul Trotter cannot even begin to define (61). Paul figures in the plot in several important ways: his having saved the life of a German youth in *The Rotters' Club* pays off in a temporary salvation of the Longbridge car plant by BMW; his sighting of Miriam Newman by a reservoir is recalled as part of Claire's identifying her sister's murderer.

Some of the links between the two novels constitute repetitions. Pamela Thurschwell has addressed this feature of Coe's writing in an essay that begins by quoting Karl Marx on the way history repeats itself—"the first time as tragedy, the second as farce" (28)—and concludes that "Marx's three interrelated topics: genre, repetition and history, raise the spectre of postmodernism, and the postmodern novel's engagement, or lack of engagement, with history and politics" (29). It can be a bit difficult to detect the farcical elements in *The Closed Circle,* even in the repetitions; it is certainly less farcical than *The Rotters' Club.* The repeated union of Benjamin and Cicely is stark and melancholy, and the Blairite "revolution"—to Coe no revolution but another repetition, this time of Thatcher-Major policies—is subject to savage rather than farcical treatment. One of Coe's repetitions is people's excitement over an election followed by disillusionment. Another, more important one, because it is symptomatic of the ruthlessness of the market system, is what happens to Steve Richards, the black former King William's student. At the very end of *The Rotters' Club* Benjamin, working rather cluelessly for a bank while awaiting university, innocently but crucially denies a loan application that would have allowed the Richards family to enlarge its fish-and-chip shop. In *The Closed Circle* Richards has become a promising engineer, despite the spoiling of his best university prospects by a malicious trickster in *The Rotters' Club,* and is headhunted by a firm called Meniscus; the asset-stripping owner of that firm (a friend of Paul's and member of the Closed Circle, as well as a lover of Claire Newman's—even those who feel kindly toward Richards are complicit in repeatedly damaging his life) shuts it down ("rationalizing"), putting Steve once again out of work.

Richards is a victim of political forces in this novel—rampant manipulation of markets by greedy, conscience-free businessmen—as he was in *The Rotters' Club,* where a more naked kind of racism blighted the promise of his young life. And politics broadly concerned is again the target of Coe's fiction. The disappointment of the Tony Blair regime, which Coe presents as nothing but a continuation of Thatcherism under another (and misleading) name, is a part of the political landscape; so is disappointment in British foreign policy. The attacks on the World Trade Center and the Pentagon on September 11, 2001, are among the macrocosmic events in *Circle,* followed by the almost inevitable move toward war against Saddam Hussein. As Thurschwell points out, this is a repetition from *What a Carve Up!*: "*The Closed Circle* finds us back once more in the realm of repetition with a president named Bush, and another Gulf War" (39, fn 3). The conflict between labor and management, which was already starting to look like an unequal fight toward the end of *The Rotter's Club,* is less important in its sequel, as the unions have lost their power (this was one of the accomplishments for which Mrs. Thatcher's admirers praise her most highly—removing the influence of powerful trade unions on British life). The auto plant at which many of the characters in the earlier book worked has become a charity case, uneconomical and viable only if the Germans choose to show pity. Its closing puts thousands of workers on the dole.

The most politically aware, or at least politically vocal, character is Douglas Anderton, who retains something of an "old Labor" mentality in his role as a newspaper columnist; even he, though, has "sold out" or at least betrayed his working-class solidarity by marrying a wealthy upper-class woman, the Honorable Francesca Gifford, the daughter of a Lord. He maintains his principles to the extent of continuing to challenge Paul Trotter, reminding him in one dinner meeting that everyone had hated Paul at school, considering him "a creepy little right-wing shit" (61). He helps to show up, by contrast, Paul's own lack of fixed beliefs or principles; after much public breast-beating on the question of going to war against Saddam Hussein, Paul eventually votes in favor for a typically selfish and unprincipled reason. The war will require his brother-in-law, a war correspondent, to leave London, thus making his apartment available again for Paul's adulteries. That people will die is of no consequence compared to his need for a convenient love nest.

Much of the political critique in *The Closed Circle* in fact revolves around the Closed Circle. This is not exactly the same group as the secret society at King William's school to which Paul was precociously named and in which he worked alongside Ronald Culpepper to rationalize the school, but it is somewhat of a continuation of it, even including the now gross and obese Culpepper. Minutes of one of its meetings are included as a counterpart to the minutes of the school group included in the earlier book. As it was once a secret society operating within the school's student body, the adult counterpart is a secret subset of another group (also founded by Paul Trotter) called the Commission for Business and Social Initiatives. The minutes include Paul's boast—rather astonishing as a comment on a Labour government, given the traditional socialist principles of a party founded by Labour unions, but probably accurate—that "private finance initiatives had now made their way into the public sector in ways which would have been unthinkable ten years ago, under the Conservative government" (206) and conclude with congratulations to Mr. Michael Usborne, CBE, who had been forced to resign from one company he had destroyed but received a handsome payoff that (later events reveal) will permit him to buy up Meniscus and close down its research division, putting 146 people, particularly including Steve Richards, out of work. The payoff he negotiates for this act of spoliation will prove so unpopular he has to move to France and hide out in a monastery.

So "the Closed Circle" in both books refers to a small hard-faced group of right-wing fanatics who exercise an inappropriate influence on events. But it has resonances far beyond that. One reviewer observed some striking numerological facts: "*The Rotters' Club* consisted of three sections of 10, 28, and 1 chapters, respectively, and the new novel's three sections have 1, 28, and 10 chapters—numbered in reverse. The circle, in other words, is closed."[30] Thinking about his growing fondness for his niece Sophie (daughter of Lois), Benjamin thinks that "perhaps some sly process of transference had taken place, unnoticed, and the affinity he had once felt for Lois was being replaced, gradually, by his growing and deepening fondness for Sophie. That would be satisfying, on some level; would have about it something of the symmetry he tended to spend much of his life vainly hunting for: the sense of a circle being closed" (252–253).

Metaphorically the closed circle may extend to the ring that permits Benjamin and Steve to identify the long-lost Harding from a photograph; or to the Rollright Stones, where Paul and his aide/girlfriend, Malvina, meet to decide on their future: "as soon as they stepped inside the circle, they were both newly conscious of a great stillness" (189); or the fact that Benjamin, at the end of the novel, is where Claire was at the beginning, "high on the chalk" at Etretat, Normandy; or "the deadlock of British politics itself."[31] Most firmly the phrase echoes in the final chapter, which once again returns to the frame anecdote, set in November 2003, that began in the opening pages of *The Rotters' Club*—Lois's daughter Sophie and Philip and Claire's son Patrick, meeting in Berlin and sharing the stories of their parents. They are in a revolving restaurant. The narrator sums up:

> And so Sophie and Patrick spent that evening telling each other stories. Sophie told the story of Harding and his anarchic schoolboy jokes; the rivalry between Richards and Culpepper; the teenage love affair between Benjamin and Cicely. And Patrick told her the story of how Benjamin and Cicely's daughter, Malvina, conceived on the morning of May 2nd, 1979—the only time they had ever made love—had unknowingly sought out her father twenty years later, only to find herself falling in love, instead, with his younger brother Paul. And he told her, too, the story of his mother, Claire, and how she had finally uncovered the truth about her sister's disappearance in the winter of 1974.
>
> As they told these stories, the platform of the restaurant revolved, and they saw the full moon go by six times, until it was almost midnight, and the smiling waiters and waitresses were standing by the door to the observation floor, waiting for them to leave. And when the full moon was hanging over the Reichstag and the Tiergarten, they knew that it was time to go, and that the circle had closed for the last time. (420)

As Philip and Lois observe their grown children, they suspect that the circle is closing in another way, their two "dynasties" joining up (428).

Patrick's account of Malvina raises the awkward question of Benjamin's attraction to his own daughter. Having met her in a bookstore, he enjoys spending time with her, and, although he rather guiltily avoids mentioning her to his wife, it never becomes an affair, in part because he introduces her to his brother, Paul, who immediately offers her a position as media adviser; eventually (after a renunciation based on his fear of bad publicity, not fidelity to his own wife), they become lovers. That she is Paul's niece is a deterrent that they choose to ignore. Earlier, Benjamin has become so close to *his* niece Sophie that, looking at her, "His heart melted" (260), and Doug Anderton asks him, "you're not seriously telling me that you've started to fancy your niece, are you? We're all getting worried about you, mate" (286). Benjamin denies fancying Sophie but unwittingly carries on into even more dubious waters by explaining, "It was the same with Malvina" (287). So: his attraction to Malvina, his unknown daughter, gives way (although not without serious pangs) to a great fondness for his niece, while his brother falls in love with his own niece, Malvina; Pamela Thurschwell refers to "Coe's fondness for incestuous, closed worlds (to the point where even choosing an apparently random sexual partner will never be truly random)" (36). Incestuous attraction may, in fact, be seen as another way of closing the circle. Each brother has an overly strong attraction to his niece, Paul's actually becoming physical.

The Closed Circle retains some of the stylistic and structural characteristics of Coe's earlier fiction up through *The Rotters' Club,* sometimes in a less striking or robust way. Music is important: Benjamin is still a composer, planning to incorporate a musical component in his never-completed novel; the phrase "high on the chalk" is an allusion to a song by the High Llamas. This group is one of Coe's favorites, and in 2008 he admitted having committed the "'sin' of combining music with the spoken word"—a plan Benjamin Trotter struggles with for two decades before giving it up—by writing a play inspired by the music of the High Llamas and designed to be performed to their music.[32] One important section is called "Norfolk Rhapsody Number 1," after a composition by the English composer Ralph Vaughan Williams. This refers to the surprising fondness of the brutal Sean Harding, in *The Rotters' Club,* for this English composer and the fact that Harding is discovered living in rural Norfolk—which is also where Claire discovers the explanation for her sister's death. The narrative also includes different textual artifacts, including letters and e-mails, songs and poems, journalism by Doug Anderton and short fiction by Malvina, minutes of meetings of the Closed Circle, passages from speeches in Parliament and magazine articles, and an entry in a hotel log-book by Harding, writing (as in *The Rotters' Club*) under the name of Arthur Pusey-Hamilton, MBE. There is some humor, although not much; again, the Pusey-Hamilton documents provide the most shocking comedy, in such passages as Sir Arthur's comments on his lady wife: "*For many weeks after she died, I could not get used to the feeling of coldness and lifelessness on her side of the bed—and it was even worse when they took the body away and buried her*" (278). The shortage of humor has political causes. Paul Gilroy comments that "Coe is often judged to be a comic, postmodern writer. His refined sense of the absurdity of contemporary political culture is attuned to the possibility that in Britain greed and selfishness have been normalized to such an extent that satire becomes effectively impossible" (198). But overall the tone of disillusionment, hopelessness, and meaninglessness prevails over any cheer. As Florence Noiville wrote, "All of Coe's disillusionment is inscribed in his titles: from *The Rotters' Club* one moves on to *The Closed Circle,* a *Bildungsroman* in which he has a character say: 'I've learned from my mistakes, and I'm sure I could repeat them perfectly'" (298). As usual in a Coe novel someone—in this case Benjamin—announces the randomness of events; having discovered the truth about the swimming-suit incident that had made him believe in Providence, he now declares, "there are no such things as miracles. Just random sets of circumstances, intersecting in ways that make no sense. . . . Just chaos. . . . Chaos and coincidence. That's all it is" (178). Also as usual, the plotting of the novel shows that, while the real world may operate in a random and chaotic fashion, Coe's fiction is quite different, making elaborate and in some ways highly improbable patterns. Consider only that, although Benjamin and Cicely have sex only once, she becomes pregnant and bears a child who seeks out her father and then becomes the partner of her uncle. The plot is carefully constructed to close circles.

That construction attracted some negative judgment from reviewers, as when Elizabeth Judd criticized its "mind-boggling coincidences and armchair analysis," even though concluding that the novel's "boundless energy and a cheerful capaciousness" redeemed these faults.[33] Steven Zeitchik, an admirer, says it has "a weakness for contrivance" (22). Reviewer Tom Lappin was more unforgiving, insisting that "There's a plot twist towards the end"—presumably the discovery that Benjamin is Malvina's father—"that would have met with substantial embarrassment before being allowed grudgingly into the script of an American daytime soap."[34] Lappin also blamed the book for crudeness, "daft" coincidences, and authorial "arrested development" and calls the novel "a dismaying shambles." This is the most severe judgment, but reviews generally were less positive than for *The Rotter's Club.* Steven Poole criticized it for "heavy portentousness" and "heavy GCSE symbolism"; in a longer, more thoughtful analysis in the *London Review of Book*s Christopher Taylor pointed to problems in the present-day setting and the disappointment of the "long delayed surprises carried over from the previous book" before admitting that the book is "strangely likeable."[35] Several of the unimpressed reviewers diagnosed hurried writing, although that does not seem to have been a problem, and others seemed dissatisfied with the fact of its being a sequel.

Naturally the novel had many admirers, as well, including Ron Charles: "There is a kind of madness in Coe's relentless pursuit of causality, of the connections between our decisions and their effects. But, as Claire suggests, looking for them is really the only sane thing to do if we hope to resist the nagging temptation to draw a circle around our interests, our desires, our lives."[36] And Richard Mason, writing in the *Independent,* fully acknowledged the strengths of this accomplished book when he praised Coe for "close attention to detail," "up-to-the-minute topicality," and, including both *The Closed Circle* and *The Rotters' Club* in his assessment, for "accomplishing that rare feat: a pair of novels that combine the addictive quality of the best soap operas with a basic cultural integrity."[37]

Jonathan Coe has always been impatient with the sterility of too many "literary novels," with the notion that popularity is always purchased at the cost of artistic integrity, that creating engaging characters and putting them to work in interesting, even complicated plots is unworthy of a real artist. In *The Rotters' Club* and *The Closed Circle,* as Mason notes, he combines the features that draw readers to popular fiction (as they draw viewers to popular television) with "cultural integrity," which must mean at least a seriousness about political developments and the prospects for British culture, and a literary artist's approach to fiction as both art and entertainment. That he has not again written books as closely linked as these two (although there are some internal links between *The Rain Before It Falls* and *Expo 58*) shows that a series—or a *roman-fleuve*—was finished after the second installment and he seems unlikely to write another.

SIX

Later Novels

The Rain Before It Falls, which appeared in 2007, was almost universally received as a stark turn away from Coe's previous pattern. Toby Lichtig may stand for most reviewers in proclaiming it "a bold departure."[1] Frances Taliaferro, writing in the *Washington Post,* began with a summary of Coe's previous work, referring to *The Rotters' Club* and *The Closed Circle* as "novels of panoramic sympathy as well as rude energy and satiric bite"; she went on to explain the difference in the new book: "In tone, it's neither ironic nor antic; in form, it's concentrated and controlled."[2] Tom Lappin not only commented on the new departure but provided a probably dubious explanation for it: "*The Rain Before It Falls* is a studied departure from nearly everything that has gone before. Coe's compelling biography of B. S. Johnson has left him with a heavy dusting of the writer's melancholy verging on misanthropy. It might be going a little too far to suggest the new novel is haunted by Johnson's baleful ghost, but certainly Coe steers a course resolutely away from his instinctive humour, and there are echoes of Johnson's nihilistic pessimism in this dark exploration of the ways in which parents can form a child, and sow the seeds of their future misery."[3]

Coe acknowledges some influence from Johnson, although not his nihilism. The biography and *The Closed Circle* were products to some extent of the same period, and, as Coe says, referring to the technique of that novel—"social realism written in the third person"—"I'd been living for many years with the voice in my head of a man who thought that kind of writing was impossible. Every time I wrote a bit of dialogue and put 'he said' after it, his voice would chip in: Oh no he didn't, you've made that up. It made me want to attempt something closer to his confessional first-person voice, the voice he uses in his novels 'Trawl' and 'The Unfortunates'. I was looking for a device that would allow me to do that."[4]

Even Coe calls this novel "the antithesis of everything I've written before, [doing] something absolutely different, either with a view to coming back and doing what I'd done before again with renewed vigour, or with a view to striking off in a new direction altogether."[5] Daniel Soar seems to have concurred, characterizing the novel as "a demonstration of what a book by him can look like when everything non-essential has been stripped away: all the pyrotechnics, all the satire, all the comedy."[6] As the comments quoted so far may indicate, critical opinion veered quite widely between those who approved of the new direction and those who thought it a mistake; Lappin, for instance, decried the construction (Coe's "device"), thought the emotional power had been dulled, and criticized "the authorial joins, the determination to hammer together a sound construction and fill in the framework with as few stylistic flourishes as possible" (18).

The device he chose was the first-person monologue of his main character, Rosamond, recorded on tape and listened to by her niece and great-nieces. This contrivance, along with the decision to limit the voice almost exclusively to that of Rosamond, helps to dictate what regular readers of Coe may miss in this new book. There is no comedy; there is no satire; there is almost no attention to politics, certainly nothing like his customary savage portrayal of Thatcherism and Blairism or Anglo-American military adventurism. Since the story begins during the Second World War, one might detect political interests in matters like the evacuation of young people from British cities, the Black Market, or the counterculture of the 1960s and 1970s, but these are so unemphatically rendered that they function more as social documentation than in any denunciatory way.

No, the issues in *The Rain Before It Falls* that may be considered political are all to do with family, sex, gender, and sexual orientation. This novel is what would undoubtedly once have been called a "woman's novel," and it is in many ways, some of them quite intricate, connected both to one of Britain's best women writers, Rosamond Lehmann, and to Virago, the women's publishers. Lehmann (1901–1990) was one of the once well-established, later somewhat overlooked female authors whose revival was partly sponsored by Virago, the press founded in 1972 by the Australian editor Carmen Callil, explicitly to "publish books which celebrated women and women's lives, and which would, by so doing, spread the message of women's liberation to the whole population and knock on the head for ever the idea that it was anything to do with burning bras or hating men."[7] When Virago published Lehmann's *The Echoing Grove* as a Virago Modern Classic in 2000, Jonathan Coe provided the introduction, as he did for *Dusty Answer*, published in 1996 (this one under the Flamingo imprint). He described *The Rain Before It Falls* as an "intended (among other things) as an *hommage*" to the Virago Modern Classics.[8]

In a conversation with John O'Connell, Coe discussed his relationship with Rosamond Lehmann, whom he describes as an "astonishing writer with a uniquely lyrical style [who was] a bestseller in the 1930s and '40s but fell out of fashion soon afterwards, languishing in obscurity" until rescued by Virago. Coe identifies his favorite of her novels as *The Ballad and the Source* (also published by Virago): "It's about a married woman who has an affair, and, under the mores of the day, loses custody of her daughter, who goes to live with her father. It's about the disasters that sets in train over three generations. My book is about a woman who has an affair and gets to keep her daughter, and the disasters that sets in train over three generations. So it's a kind of reply to 'The Ballad and the Source,' and my character Rosamond (who's named after Lehmann) is close to Sybil Jardine, its dominant matriarchal figure."[9]

There is more: Rosamond's cousin Beatrix (the woman who gets to keep her daughter) is named for Rosamond Lehmann's sister. Chris Lehmann points to some of the other elements of Coe's *hommage.* Beatrix's mother is called Ivy, an echo of Ivy Compton-Burnett, "another Virago author" who "specialized in novels largely made up of icy, petulant intrafamily dialogue." Rosamond and Beatrix, in the novel, perform as extras in a film called *Gone to Earth,* which was based on a novel of that name written by Mary Webb—another Virago author. Were it not common for Coe to build in subtle references to his admired influences, one might automatically dismiss Lehmann's most obscure connection, but it is possible. That is, a particularly nasty review of *The Echoing Grove* (to which Coe wrote the introduction, of course) was written by Brendan Gill in the *New Yorker,* and Rosamond's niece is named Gill: "it is surely no accident that Coe constructs its action so that a character named Rosamond is patiently, emotionally and . . . dramatically instructing a character named Gill in the true workings of destiny."[10]

What is the point of this intricate linkage to Rosamond Lehmann? Coe has often explained what attracted him to Lehmann and the Virago Modern Classics. In a tellingly entitled essay, "My Literary Love Affair," he writes about *The Ballad and the Source,* his favorite among Lehmann's works: "It's a story of the relationship between a mother, her daughter and her granddaughters, in which betrayal, manipulation and emotional histrionics are shown to have a cumulatively destructive effect across generations. It is indeed melodramatic—although, as someone who has always seen life itself as being full of melodrama, I simply find that this adds to its realism."[11] In the same article he attributes to his discovery of the Virago list his decision to write what became his first published novel about a woman. None of his novels between *An Accidental Woman* and *The Rain Before It Falls* has a woman as its central character, although women are treated with great insight and sympathy as secondary characters in, say, *What a Carve Up!* and *The Rotters' Club* and Sarah is one of the focal figures in *The House of Sleep,* where, by the way, the main male character becomes a woman.

In his introduction to *Dusty Answer,* Coe writes:

> A peculiar characteristic of Rosamond Lehmann's novels, finally, is their uncompromising capacity for making the reader feel gendered. While it

> would be far too simple to say that women like them and men don't, it is true that reader responses to these books tend to divide up along gender lines. . . . To consider where this leave male readers—indeed, to investigate the whole process of cross-gender identification among readers of fiction—would doubtless consume (and must already have consumed) numerous hefty volumes of literary theory: so I shall confine myself to a simpler and more personal point, which is that one of the things that appeals to me the most strongly about Rosamond Lehmann's novels is their superb portrayals of men.[12]

This is suggestive. Coe is himself a refutation of any simple declaration that men don't like Lehmann's novels; he clearly distrusts the notion of "women's fiction" at least insofar as it is supposed to limit both the subject matter available to the novelist and the gender of the readership; and it is undoubtedly a reliable inference from his praise of Lehmann that he would like to be the kind of male writer capable of superb portrayals of women. (He has declared not only that his household is female, consisting aside from him of a wife, two daughters, and two female cats, but also that "I don't see why literature should be gender-bound, I think it is a writer's duty to have empathy with both sexes, I can't just ignore one half of humanity.")[13] His success in this task in *The Rain Before It Falls* was variously judged, as we shall see.

Efforts to provide "a cause" for Coe's turning to a different subject matter or approach in his fiction—whether his reading of Rosamond Lehmann, his years of immersion in B. S. Johnson, or some sort of reaction against humor and satire—are reductive, and yet there is one more to consider, his own family situation. *The Rain Before It Falls* is a novel about family, and particularly about daughters. His own two daughters, born in 1997 and 2000, respectively, presumably have no more in common with Rosamond and Beatrix than being three years apart in age, but becoming the father of daughters is likely to foreground daughterhood as a subject matter.

For most of his career (the major exception, up to this point, coming in *The Dwarves of Death*) Jonathan Coe has used a somewhat relaxed, third-person heterodiegetic narrative technique with selective omniscience. *The Rain Before It Falls* begins the same way: "When the telephone rang Gill was outside."[14] The next few pages, which detail Gill's attendance at the funeral of her aunt Rosamond, tell us that she was alarmed by moments of detachment, that her husband had an obscure sense of having failed her, that her brother David had never known whether to believe Gill's account of clairvoyant episodes: in other words, although the characters are seen from without and their actions related in the third person, the narrator freely dips into one consciousness after another. This does not prevent Gill from continuing to be the focal character.

But this is just the frame. It reveals that Gill discovers evidence that Rosamond had killed herself, apparently while listening to a recording of *Songs of the Auvergne* by Joseph Canteloube (a significant detail). She left a set of tape recordings, instructing Gill to get it to Imogen, who, in a flashback, is seen to have been a young blind girl Gill met once at Rosamond's house in London. A few other important narrative points in this introduction include Gill's recollection of a drive in France, years before, when she killed a blackbird with her car and saw it as an ominous omen, implying a death in the family, and the sequel to Rosamond's instructions, which was disappointing, because, despite all efforts, Imogen was untraceable. So, on a trip to London to visit her own daughters, Catharine and Elizabeth (also three years apart, like Rosamond and Beatrix, like the Coe daughters), Gill decides to listen to the tapes with her daughters. There is an interlude a bit more than halfway through the book and a bit more than halfway through the tapes when the present-day situation and the third-person narration resume: Gill, Elizabeth, and Catharine go to a London church for a concert in which Catharine, a music student, is performing.

The function of this interruption seems at least threefold. The story being told by Rosamond on the tapes has come to a crisis, and the "present-day" London interlude provides a brief spell of distraction and hence suspense. It shows a mother who loves her daughters and is loved by them (a sharp contrast to the story unreeling on the tapes); listening to Catharine's performance, Gill "knew that they had never been so close to each other" (131–132). And Catharine's performance demonstrates something about art and about (a regular concern with Coe) the interpenetration of narrative and music, as Gill realizes that the music Gill is playing—on a flute and with electronic feedback—"was a soundtrack: the soundtrack to a story they had heard together only a few hours earlier, about two little girls, running away from home, on a winter's night in wartime Shropshire. . . . These images, these fitful, antique images, were somehow inscribed into the fabric of her music. Gill could not have been more convinced of the fact, even if her daughter had been trying to describe the scene in words" (132).

That last comment links back to the tapes themselves, as they record an effort by Rosamond to describe in words, for a blind woman, twenty photographs. The three women resume the listening project, which gives way, at the very end of the novel, to a short chapter of interior monologue and a final chapter of third-person narration focused on Gill, with a long epistolary interpolation.

Rosamond's narration, which is in effect a tape-recorded letter to Imogen to explain her family history and her own fate, is in one sense a regular homodiegetic, "first-person" narrative, but Coe has artfully arranged it so that it is also a set of twenty short chapters, each one ostensibly describing a photograph but in fact using the photographs and their regular chronological advance toward Rosamond's present, as occasion for a quantum of the story of Imogen, her mother, and her grandmother. As a first-person narrative, the main part of the novel, then, is crucially dependent on Rosamond. How successful is that dependence?

Tom Lappin excoriates it, declaring this "variant on the epistolary novel has Rosamond regaling Imogen with her family history through a meticulous description of 20 faded photographs. It's a baffling conceit, turning Rosamond into a kind of geriatric Nick Hornby, distilling her life down to a Top 20" (18). Erica Wagner, who calls the novel a failure, explains, "Pictures are described, but they never come to life; and because the great majority of the book takes place in Rosamond's haphazard, randomly judgmental memory, the conversations that might have enlivened it are almost entirely absent."[15] The reviewer in the *Atlantic Monthly* disagreed, disdaining the "twenty photographs" structure but reckoning that the style, "well-suited to his protagonist, is dignified and sure, often almost dry in its directness."[16] Without question Rosamond's voice and tone are very different from Jonathan Coe's usual ones; he has undertaken something very challenging in this book, to depict a rather terrible story through the focus on an observer who is quite ordinary, not in her history, not in her moral complexity, but in her personality and her "literary" style—which is not a *literary* style but a conversational one. Rosamond has worked in publishing but is not a writer.

It is true that from time to time her descriptive efforts rise to something like poetic prose; describing scenery from her beloved rural Shropshire, she says:

> The gorse and the purple heather are unchanging, and so are the sheep-tracks which cut through them and criss-cross them, the twisted rocky outcrops which surprise you at every turn, the warm browns of the bracken, the distant greys of the conifer plantations, tucked far away down in secretive valleys. You cannot put a price on the sense of freedom and timelessness that is granted to you there, as you stand on the high ridge beneath a flawless sky of April blue and look across at the tame beauties of the English countryside, to the east, and to the west a hint of something stranger—the beginnings of the Welsh mountains, already hinted at by one of the wilder and more eerie features of the Long Mynd itself. (84–85)

This is able and evocative description. As for the difficulty of describing photographs vividly, this is a problematic undertaking anyway, as Rosamond herself acknowledges from time to time. Telling a blind girl what something looks like is never going to be easy.

The first-person narrator is always subject to some scrutiny on grounds of reliability. Does Rosamond tell her story fairly and accurately? Are her judgments ones that readers are encouraged to share? Are there unacknowledged motives at work within her that the novel invites us to suspect? Some readers think the answer to this question is yes. Sophie Harrison considers the characterization of her voice "a little too easy, and not quite consistent" and suggests that "its authenticity and veracity matter terribly."[17] The inconsistency she detects may be what Patrick Ness diagnoses when he says that Rosamond's voice is usually "a lovely thing," with language that is "simple direct, yet often quite chilling," while considering her final words "too woolly for the tough, shrewd woman who's gone before."[18] Ian McGillis claims that the story "sets up uneasy questions about Rosamond. Her motives at first appear honorable, even noble, but how much of what she presents as compassion might actually be something more self-serving and manipulative?"[19] (It is worth noting that Rosamond herself wonders if she should be telling Imogen the worst news, that she was blinded by her own mother.) And David Robson calls Rosamond a "not-quite-reliable narrator, a lesbian with frustrated maternal instincts."[20] This is a little puzzling; both her lesbianism and her frustrated maternal instincts are openly announced, and it is hard to see how they derange her judgment or mislead the reader.

Coe's comment on this same question, provided to a German reading group, is instructive: "The irony in the story is that the only good mother is Rosamond. But she could not be a mother, having discovered early on in her life that she was gay, and back then adoption wasn't open to gay couples."[21] Her cousin Beatrix, having used Rosamond for years, having left her daughter for Rosamond to care for while she pursues a man to Canada, having exploited her in every possible way, finally separates them cruelly by believing, or pretending to believe, that Rosamond has lesbian designs on Thea.

Daniel Soar is one critic who has devoted considerable attention to the theme of lesbianism in *Rain* as well as in Coe's other novels. He identifies Dorothy Winshaw from *What a Carve Up!* as lesbian (because she is forceful, cruel, and contemptuous of her husband), then suggests that "there's no narrative reason for Dorothy to be a dyke, and the idea is taken nowhere. She's gay [or Soar concludes that she is] because it happens to be funnier that way . . . there are a good number of dykey women in Coe's work as a whole" (32). Soar includes lesbians among some other elements that recur in Coe's fiction, because, he thinks, Coe is compelled to include them: "contradicting the structural rigour are all those elements—the lesbians, the photographs, the music (there's a lot of music)—that have no formal reason to exist but insert themselves, non-disruptively, nonetheless: a remembered image of castle-building on a beach, a Shropshire lane, a brief replayed flirtation in a black-and-white film. These things are there because the novelist likes them, and can't avoid them" (32).

This is a puzzling criticism. Consider the fact that several elements he mentions are very important, that is, they have a very good formal reason to exist: one example is the castle-building on the beach in *The House of Sleep,* which plays a crucial role in the plot that divides and unites Robert and Sarah. Similarly, music is not just a quirky Jonathan Coe compulsion; in *The Rain Before It*

Falls, Songs of the Auvergne functions symbolically and psychologically. There are, admittedly, recurrent elements in Coe's fiction, but the lesbianism of Rosamond can be explained in several ways that do not require authorial compulsion. One is that there are lesbians in the world, so to include one in one's novel need not require much justification. Veronica in *The House of Sleep* is also a lesbian: she can be more open in the 1980s about her needs than Rosamond could in the 1950s and 1960s, and that novel includes a young girl who is the daughter of a lesbian couple, including Sarah's old lover Veronica. This is the other important reason for making Rosamond a lesbian (Coe explains this himself)—in this ongoing, multigenerational story of mothers damaging their daughters, the best prospect for breaking the cycle would be for Rosamond to adopt Thea or, failing that, Thea's daughter, Imogen, but neither course is open to a lesbian. And Rosamond's frank but hardly sensational explanation of her lesbianism is necessary as part of the accounting she tries to provide Imogen, that is, how life turned out as it did for the unloved blind girl.

Rosamond's lesbianism and childlessness are important parts of a long family tragedy. Coe might be glossing Philip Larkin's famous poem about intergenerational damage, "This Be the Verse," which coldly declares that parents pass along misery to the next generation, unintentionally but inevitably; Larkin's final suggested remedy is "And don't have any kids yourself."[22] But although childlessness may preserve Rosamond from transmitting the misery that her cousins Beatrix and Thea hand on to their daughters, it can hardly appear here as a happy solution to the destructiveness of family life.

Helpless repetition is the problem here. Beatrix is mistreated by her mother, who favors her sons and even her dogs and is a cold and selfish parent; in part because of this Beatrix makes an early escape into sex and an unsuitable marriage and, just as selfishly, abandons her daughter Thea in order to fulfill her own desires. In due course Thea turns to a worthless man, blinds her daughter, Imogen, and loses custody of her when she is imprisoned. When last seen, Imogen seems as if she might be breaking the chain of damage, perhaps because she has been adopted by a different sort of family—as Larkin recommends, she is getting out as early as she can, even if her extrication is hardly by her own agency. The narrator of Lehmann's *The Ballad and the Source*, an acknowledged intertext for *The Rain Before It Falls*, says of a similar family situation, "A terrible echo stirred. This same paternal threat, expressed in even direr terms—I had heard it only a short while ago from the lips of another child. It seemed that this thing went on and on, like a curse. Liar begot liar; and all their road, forward and back, far back, was cratered with disastrous pits of guilt, haunted by ruinous voices crying vengeance."[23]

The connection with Lehmann's novel is one aspect of Coe's intertexuality, which is a persistent feature of his fiction. (The narrator of Lehmann's novel has a relationship with a girl a few years older that is similar to Rosamond's with Beatrix.) He is a linking novelist, finding connections in surprising places. The title of the novel comes from a tune performed by the vibraphonist Gary Burton and composed by Michael Gibbs; the introductory author's note says that "The description of Catharine's music is inspired by the work of Theo Travis on his album *Slow Life*." The most important music actually incorporated into the text of the book is *Songs of the Auvergne* by Joseph Canteloube. This is the record on the turntable when Rosamond ends her life (the local doctor finds it still playing when she comes in and discovers the body). Why does it mean so much to Rosamond? This is explained in the chapter devoted to photograph number twelve, a picture taken in the Auvergne, showing Rebecca, the love of Rosamond's life, and Thea, at age six or seven. This is the height of their happiness as a family: by the end of the chapter, Thea has been reclaimed by Beatrix and Rebecca has abandoned Rosamond. But this is the most beautiful and happy spell in the novel. The explanation is that Rebecca and Rosamond had been listening to *Songs of the Auvergne* on the radio and "became rather amorous with each other" (138). "Afterwards, for both of us, those songs were forever associated with that occasion, but more than that, somehow they became—what is the word?—symbolic?—or do I mean *totemic*?—totemic, I think—of the love between us. There was one song in particular, one of the most famous ones—'Bailero,' it is called, a most beautiful love song, very slow, and very sad—it starts with the woodwind voicing such plangent phrases, while the violins play long, lovely, shimmering chords, and then the soprano's voice enters so unexpectedly, so dramatically, singing this extraordinarily *melancholy* tune" (138).

The music inspires the vacation in the Auvergne, and the music at the end of her life is a tribute to the love she shared with Rebecca. Coe may be insistently fond of musical references, but this is wholly functional in the economy of the novel, with its tribute to love and even the introduction of the melancholy, which in the same chapter will occur on the level of event.

Film, too, has always played an important role in Coe's work. The way it works in this novel is unusual and daring. The movie in question, *Gone to Earth*, is a 1950 film by Michael Powell, based on a novel by Mary Webb and set in Shropshire. It was filmed in Much Wenlock, and, in Coe's use of it, Beatrix, living with her unsatisfactory husband in Much Wenlock, arranges for Rosamond and herself to be extras. Rosamond describes the shot very carefully, with "Beatrix and me, standing in the left-hand corner of the frame, laughing and talking together" (94). On she goes, describing their clothing and the street action behind them. This is in fact a perfectly accurate account of the scene in Powell's film, which readers can watch for themselves, so that Coe has put his fictional characters into a real film, replacing the actual extras, whoever they were. Two connections come from this. One is that Beatrix begins an affair with a carpenter on the set and, when the filming is over, runs away with him, taking her daughter with her, for three years of traveling around Ireland in a gipsy caravan.

The other result is one of those scenes that might actually qualify as the kind of repeated element Soar mentions as disrupting the formal rigor of the fiction: in this case a scene where a child sees a movie, or part of one, to the dismay of its parents. Here Rosamond remembers seeing Jennifer Jones in *Duel in the Sun,* "and I think my parents regretted taking me to see it from the moment the credits rolled" (89). That she fantasizes about Jennifer Jones rather than Gregory Peck is one early suggestion of the direction her erotic life will take. A similar event concerns the young Michael Owen, in *What a Carve Up!,* who sees the film of that name on a rainy holiday Sunday, only to have his viewing aborted when his mother takes him out of the theater, having realized he is fascinated by looking at Shirley Eaton in her slip. Other repeated elements here are caravans (Rosamond points out their frequent reappearance in her photos and thus her narrative) and geography. Rosamond's family lives in the southern inner suburbs of Birmingham, like a very large number of Coe's characters, and Beatrix's family lives in rural Shropshire, like Coe's grandparents.

What does it all mean? Is it enough to provide a panoply of misfortune? Is there a pattern to these events? Rosamond thinks there is: she claims (speaking to Imogen, of course), "There is a reason for everything, in case you haven't learned it yet, in your short life. In fact, the story I am trying to tell you will demonstrate as much—if I tell it properly" (45). Later she speaks of Imogen's "inevitability." Rosamond herself wonders if after death she and Rebecca will be reunited and "sitting side by side again, in the meadow above the little shingle beach" (221)—in other words, in the Auvergne—and recursive patterns seem to endorse the meaningfulness of events in the plot in a way quite different from the way that most of Coe's earlier books have a moment when someone, perhaps the narrator, announces the absolute randomness and meaninglessness of events. That this occurs in the middle of a very elaborately contrived plot, often with almost unbelievable linkages and coincidences, is thought-provoking. The main narrator of *The Rain Before It Falls,* at least, insists that everything happens for a reason. And this is in the context of a plot with fewer coincidences than the usual Coe novel. One is that as a child Beatrix earns her mother's murderous hatred by letting a dog run away, entirely unexpectedly and innocently; later, at the very end of the novel, Thea reveals that Imogen is dead and that "she was out in the park with her brothers one morning, taking that dog for a walk. And apparently, although it had never done anything like this before, the dog suddenly ran off, barking, into the road, and Imogen heard him and ran off after him" (237). It is almost as if she was trying to make good, unwittingly, her grandmother's inability to retrieve the dog. Gill realizes that Imogen's death took place when she hit the blackbird, in France, and had a premonition of a death in the family; she concludes that "Nothing was random, after all. There was a pattern: a pattern to be found somewhere" (238).

Is this enough? Adam Mars-Jones thought not, declaring that "It's hard to know how seriously to take this rather half-hearted suggestion of mysterious forces at work."[24] He was one of the fairly large number of reviewers disappointed with *The Rain Before It Falls.* The tendency to cite the strengths of *What a Carve Up!* or *The House of Sleep* before pointing to the comparative weaknesses of *Rain* suggests that for some, at least, Coe's decision to do something very different was unwelcome. Patrick Ness thought that the book had "too much tragedy, finally. The last revelations are so grim that credibility starts to strain" (16), and Daniel Soar, in a long essay that contrasted *Rain* with *The House of Sleep* and *What a Carve Up!,* wrote of "the flabbiness of the writing" and concluded (with a witty allusion to *What a Carve Up!*) that "Unfortunately, *The Rain Before It Falls* lacks the necessary brio" (33).

What it does have is a kind of unflinching honesty; a willingness to center its story on and hand over the narrative duties to an unremarkable and not even very eloquent woman; and some of the traits for which Coe praises Rosamond Lehmann: "an astonishing, unembarrassed emotionality that gives a visceral power to her recurring themes—thwarted love, faithlessness, the unbearable sadness of naïve romantic feelings being crushed by the passage of time."[25]

The next novel, *The Terrible Privacy of Maxwell Sim,* was not, like *The Rain Before It Falls,* devoid of humor; it contains some comic elements, many of them at the expense of the protagonist, and there is a modest amount of satire on twenty-first-century developments in society, mostly electronic inventions for more efficient communication, which paradoxically separate one person from another. These are not the main point of the book, though, nor do they prevent it from being, on the whole, rather sad.

Instead, *Terrible Privacy* is a kind of omnibus of several types of narrative. One is the shaggy-dog story, that is, one in which the failure of the plot to deliver its expected conclusion is part of the novelist's aim. Another is a road novel; another is a sort of coming-of-age story, despite the protagonist being forty-eight years old when he begins seriously to learn about himself. There is a very serious *hommage* to B. S. Johnson, both in the inclusion of certain plot elements and in the metafictional devices employed, particularly at the end of the novel. And Coe explores the possibilities of fictional form in a more complex way than he had done since *The House of Sleep.*

One reviewer made the effort to link *The Terrible Privacy of Maxwell Sim* with some of the author's past work, including several "state-of-the-nation" novels: "But in *The Terrible Privacy of Maxwell Sim,* he departs. Here is something that undoubtedly has the feel of a state-of-the-nation novel. But it isn't any of the things I describe above [an urban comedy with a wide sweep and representative characters]: it has no geographical centre, it's framed (flashbacks aside) by a single long car-journey, and it's interested in one character and one character only. Most of all, although it's a comic novel, it's not a comedy. If I understand Coe's project rightly, this is a state-of-the-nation novel for an age where that sort of book can no longer be written."[26]

This is the first of Coe's novels to be named after a character. That Maxwell Sim (called Max, usually, and with a surname that, he recognizes, is reminiscent of the SIM card of a mobile phone) is so unimpressive constitutes part of the author's achievement. William Giraldi, reviewing the novel, connected Max to the "manifold misfits in the work of Jonathan Coe," explaining that "Coe's protagonists are adept at throwing themselves away, making themselves ostracized and obsolete with either imbecility, or melancholy, or hubris, or some crafty combination."[27] Coe has discussed the selection, or creation, of Maxwell Sim. Linking him to Michael Owen of *What a Carve Up!* because both are passive figures, he wrote, "thinking about it, seven out of my nine novels feature or are narrated by passive, slightly depressed men—often failed writers or composers or both—who show a rather uncommitted sexuality and tend to fixate on past romantic disappointments. The hero of my latest, *The Terrible Privacy of Maxwell Sim,* is a textbook example."[28] It is much more than a representative example; in fact, he is the *extreme* instance: he is far more passive, more disappointing—and disappointed—romantically, and more depressed than his fellows. Max is not a failed artist; if anything, he is a failed employee in the returns department of a toy store, following which he is a failed temporary participant in a publicity stunt for a toothbrush company. His wife has left him, and his few lurching efforts at romantic involvement in the course of the novel are utterly misguided. And he is not "slightly depressed": as the novel begins he is finishing a six-month medical leave from his job for clinical depression. Most important, perhaps, he is the least intelligent and least literate protagonist Coe has employed.

Thinking back on his marriage to Caroline, a restless wife and aspiring author, he admits he was never in her league, intellectually. He cannot understand her ideas about books, for instance, although he did once ask her for some suggested reading: "She told me to try some contemporary American fiction. 'Like what' I asked. 'Try getting one of the Rabbit books' [that is, the series by John Updike from *Rabbit Run* to *Rabbit at Rest*], she told me, and a few hours later, when I came back from the bookshop and showed her what I'd bought, she said, 'is this meant to be some sort of joke?' It was *Watership Down.*" Having bought Richard Adams's 1972 adventure novel about talking rabbits, Max does reflect, "(Bloody good book, actually, if you ask me. Didn't change my life, though.)"[29]

Coe told one interviewer it was a "joy to write about someone so ordinary . . . to see the world from the point of view of somebody who wasn't particularly imaginative and wasn't particularly well educated."[30] Max is aware of his shortcomings. Early in the novel he admits he isn't very good at describing people; he then goes on, "I am not very good at describing clothes either—are you looking forward to the next 300 pages?" (7).

Max is not just uneducated, incurious, and parochial (he thinks Watford, England, is a fine place and enjoys eating at motorway restaurants). He is also nearly friendless; he has one work "friend" named Trevor, his best friend from childhood is estranged from him, and he has seventy friends on Facebook, "most of them complete strangers" (19). His mother is dead, and his father, living a world away in Australia, is virtually a stranger to him. After six months off work and a month away in Australia, he comes home to find no personal letters, five telephone messages, and more than a hundred e-mails, all but one of which are advertisements for impotence remedies and "male enhancement." On the flight from Australia, he makes an effort to promote human contact with the man sitting next to him on the airplane and delivers a long and boring monologue—what Jonathan Darbyshire calls "a pitch-perfect rendition of the manic garrulousness of the lonely"—only to find that his new "friend" is silent because he has been dead for five or ten minutes.[31]

His most intimate relationship as the novel begins is with his ex-wife, but even this is made possible only through a dishonest stratagem; he creates a false identity for himself in order to join Mumsnet, a discussion website for mothers, on which, posing as a woman, he discovers that in fourteen years of marriage, "I can honestly say that she never, ever wrote to me—or even addressed me—with the kind of affection she showed to 'Liz Hammond' in that first email" (88).[32] He later falls in love with his car's on-board computer system, or its voice. His daughter considers him hopeless.

What are readers to make of Maxwell Sim? From one perspective it is possible to claim him as a victim of modern life. He tends in this direction himself, pointing to conditions that would, if taken very seriously, help to qualify the novel as a "state-of-the-nation" text: the state of a nation in which people interact only through the Internet, sitting together at dining tables but spending their time texting to absent correspondents rather than speaking in full human presence. The financial crisis of 2008–2009 also figures, with business failures and the threat of joblessness present.

But this diagnosis is too easy. Max does not cope well with twenty-first-century life, but others do. He is his own worst enemy. The reviewer William Giraldi provides the sternest account of Max's ethical failures: "As for Max's moral core, it has rotted through. He half-heartedly attempted to maim his best friend's child because he was envious of the boy's freedom, and he impersonates a woman online in order to chat with his estranged wife. The misfits of Barbusse, Dostoevsky and Camus might be murderers, perverts and misanthropes, but they are also intellectually charismatic. Maxwell Sim is not even interesting enough for scorn." Some might find his posing as Liz Hammond more pathetic than outrageous, and his assault on the friend's son consists of shoving him into some stinging nettles rather than maiming him, but the basic diagnosis is correct. Maxwell Sim is envious, baffled, clueless, and, most important, terribly unaware of himself. (That his wife likes him better as a woman may be a clue to his own radical sexual maladjustment.)

To build a novel about such a protagonist takes some self-assurance; not every reader found it successful. Chris Barton balanced calling Max "not very bright and generally weak in a way that makes him frustrating" with thinking him "often amusing company"; Alex Clark recognized him as the type of person every reader dreads becoming, "an immediately recognizable type, both literary and social, a Pooterish chronicler of daily life, entrapped by minutiae and unable to fathom their wider significance. Resolutely prosaic"; Sam Leith calls him a "self-hating and incurious dullard."[33] Ed Park points out that he is a "tricky creation: a nonwriter, with zero interest in books, who is writing his own story," and we are very early on notified that Max sympathizes with those who have to read it (although, in fairness, later on he comes to believe he is getting the hang of writing. Readers must form their own opinion.).[34] Max's characteristics and his obvious blindness to important facts about himself identify him very quickly as an unreliable narrator. As Leo Robson noticed, the early part of the book carefully differentiates him from his creator, as he reveals an indifference to both literature and politics; Max also "uses the phrase 'as far as I could see,' a little nudging joke from the author because this character will show numerous signs of myopia and delusion."[35]

What, then, is the aim of such a central creation? Coe has given two related explanations. One is that "I was hoping to make him a kind of Everyman . . . as ordinary as possible: an ordinary man, doing an ordinary job in an ordinary town."[36] This might hint at some doctrinaire realism, insisting on a slice of life, an "ordinary mind on an ordinary day," as recommended by Virginia Woolf in her 1921 essay "Modern Fiction."[37] Most readers, at least, have found Sim an unsatisfactory Everyman, because he is below the average, inferior to the ordinary. But Coe has also called the book an effort to find "strangeness at the heart of the deeply ordinary," insisting that "If you look hard enough you can find romance and mystery and dark undercurrents everywhere in life—even in the most unprepossessing places, the Park Inn Hotel, Watford, or the café at Knutsford services, and I suppose doing that has—to put it rather grandly—become one of my mission statements as a writer."[38]

This comes closer to accounting for the effect of Maxwell Sim. Readers are not being invited to read three hundred pages about a deeply ordinary man in order to discover how deeply ordinary he is; they are being given views, through his ordinariness and *around the edges of* his incurious and un-self-aware narration, of darkness, and romance, and mystery. The quality of those helps to justify—or, for those who find Max's ordinariness and moral myopia irredeemable, does *not* justify—Coe's dedication of his novel to a character less obviously engaging than any he has used before; this effect is redoubled since Max is the first-person narrator, so that the narration itself lacks the kind of wit, artful allusion, and brio that one expects from a Jonathan Coe narrator.

It is true that Max's account is varied or interspersed with four other narratives written by other hands and spoken by other narrators. In this the novel is reminiscent of *A Touch of Love:* in that book, readers remember, the story of unhappy postgraduate Robin is narrated by a third-person omniscient narrator, but in four places that narrative gives way to short stories written by Robin. In *Terrible Privacy* the overall narrative, entrusted to Maxwell himself, pauses four times to give way to documents that he encounters. The first is "WATER: The Misfit," an account of a failed yachtsman, Donald Crowhurst, written by a man named Clive, the uncle of a young woman (Poppy) whom Max meets on the way home from Australia. Although initially it is little more than an interesting tale about a sad man's decline in the 1960s, both Crowhurst and Clive will become more important in Max's life. Chapter 2 contains "EARTH: The Nettle Pit," and its provenance is even more indirect and yet telling. Max's ex-wife, Caroline, has sent it to "Liz Hammond," her correspondent on Mumsnet; she is unaware that Liz Hammond is Max, who is the main character in the story, lightly fictionalized. It tells of his envy of his friend Chris, which has led to his pushing Chris's son into a nettle pit. The last line of Caroline's story is very perceptive (although, as Max never comments on it, one cannot say whether he recognizes the perception): "she saw him as a man surrendering to a feeling that must have come so naturally, with such a healing inevitability, that it might almost have felt like a release; a man in mourning over the death of the son he had always wanted" (131).

"FIRE: The Folded Photograph" appears in a collection of old documents that Mr. and Mrs. Byrne, family friends, entrust to Max to deliver to their daughter Alison, owner of the papers, whom he will see in Edinburgh. He serendipitously discovers this essay, an old college assignment of Alison's, which recounts a family vacation the Sims and the Byrnes took together and Alison's disturbing reaction to Max's apparently creepy father, who had taken a photograph of her and Chris (the same friend who appears in "The Nettle Pit"). Alison discovers Mr. Sim in the obvious aftermath of masturbation and with the photograph folded so that "the figure of Chris was hidden and the only person you could see was me, all wet and cold in my skimpy orange bikini" (181).

Characteristically, in a life of missed opportunities, Max reads the story as revealing how he had missed his chance with Alison, who had worn the bikini to try to catch his attention; later, spending the night at her home, he misses yet another opportunity with Alison, as he ignores her increasingly blunt hints that she would welcome him in her bed, concluding with "I've got a feeling I'm wasting my time here, but just in case, Max, I'm going to leave my bedroom door open" (242). Instead, he reads the last interpolated narrative.

And that story, "AIR: The Rising Sun," is the most important of them. In a binder of poems written by his father, which Max had collected while clearing out his father's flat, he discovers "The Rising Sun: A Memoir." Although thinking "I wasn't going to like what I found in there," Max reads it anyway. It is an explanation of his father's relationship with a man named Roger Anstruther, a magnetic and charismatic figure to whom Mr. Sim was devoted in his single days. It is clear that the relationship was homosexual, and the conclusion, built on an ironic misunderstanding, explains how Maxwell came to be and how his parents married. Having made a momentous decision—"I could no longer fight what I knew to be my destiny. I could no longer tell myself lies about my own nature" (273)—in other words, to abandon his "low-key, chaste, and uneventful courtship" (272) of Barbara, a limited blonde secretary who shares none of his cultural interests, and own his homosexual desire—he sets off to meet Roger at the Rising Sun, a favorite pub. There are two pubs called the Rising Sun, however, so they miss each other; he gets drunk, sleeps with Barbara, and impregnates her. Hence his marriage and hence the birth of Maxwell Sim, after a drunken, frustrated, and unintentional reaction to the frustration of gay longing. No wonder his parents had been so ill matched. Max remembers Roger Anstruther visiting his home, and he realizes that his father had folded the photograph not to exclude Chris from view and single out Alison but the reverse.

While gathering his father's effects in Lichfield, Max has discovered a poem called "Two Duets"; a neighbor relates it to T. S. Eliot's *Four Quartets,* which of course Max has never heard of, although he is aware enough to recognize Eliot as the librettist for *Cats.* Miss Erith explains: "They're all themed around the four elements—air, earth, fire and water. Your father was a great admirer of Eliot's" (195). The father is responsible for only one of the quartets, although the most important, and they appear here in reverse order from Miss Erith's accounting.

This is an indication of the artful form of this novel. Its subject—a dull man who becomes less dull, partly through an extreme reaction to his situation that lands him in the hospital and partly through a long-delayed recognition of who and what he is—can seem quite mundane. It is energized and complicated, in a satisfying way, by Coe's innovative methodology.

One part of this is the use of a plot that is fundamentally a road narrative, with other material that deepens its effect. Maxwell Sim, coming off a medical leave for depression and not keen about returning to his job, gets an opportunity to help with the launch of a new product, an environmentally responsible toothbrush. The company's slogan, "We Reach Furthest," suggests a public relations exercise. Lindsay, the PR specialist, having asked Max, "what do *you* think is the best kind of story, Max?"—to which Max, already taking what readers will see, long before Maxwell will, as a fruitless erotic interest in Lindsay, replies "hopefully": "Boy meets girl?"—she corrects him saying that it is a *quest:* "The journey. The voyage of discovery" (101). The plan is for four men to take off from Reading in Berkshire, the company headquarters, in Toyota Priuses, for the four most distant places in Great Britain in each direction. Max is chosen to go north, which is the longest drive, and is to drive to the Shetland Islands, carrying sample toothbrushes and a video camera for a video diary. The car is equipped, significantly, with what the British call a Satnav (GPS in American usage).

Max's aim in the quest is quite different from the company's, including visiting his ex-wife and daughter and old friends (including Alison) as well as stopping off in Lichfield to clear his father's apartment. He mostly forgets to turn on the video camera to make a video diary; he stalls and delays and eventually exasperates his supervisors by his failure to fulfill his mission.

Finally he reaches Scotland but becomes increasingly disoriented and troubled. Along the way he has named his onboard computer, or Satnav, Emma and fallen in love with her, and his dialogue with her becomes, or seems to him to become, two-way, with Emma asking him questions and delivering wisdom. He has a complete breakdown. The result is revealed in a news article from the *Aberdeenshire Press and Journal,* which appears as a sort of epigraph before the novel properly begins and reveals, among other details, that the police found Maxwell drunk, unconscious, and naked, suffering from hypothermia in a car abandoned in the snow. "The mystery deepened as the policemen inspected the boot of the car and found two cardboard boxes containing more than 400 toothbrushes, as well as a large black bin liner filled with picture postcards of the Far East" (n.p.) The other significant fact is that Guest Toothbrushes, Max's employer, had failed and gone into liquidation the morning he was found.

Max's quest, then, is a failure from the point of view of Guest Toothbrushes; it is mostly a failure from Max's point of view, since his efforts to reunite with his wife or regain closeness with his daughter come to nothing, and even his chance with Alison is derailed by his stealing away in the early morning. He succeeds in clearing his father's apartment: the postcards mentioned in the newspaper report are the result (they are from Roger Anstruther to Max's father). From another point of view, unavailable to Max himself, the quest is successful; he reaches goals he had never set, discovers truths about his father, and makes some progress toward discovering truths about himself.

A quest narrative is customarily linear, and Max's does move him from Reading to the Grampian region of Scotland. But alongside it is a circular one. The novel begins, after all, with Max in Australia on Valentine's Day 2009, sitting in a restaurant and watching a Chinese woman and her daughter, who impress him because they are happy and fully engaged with each other: he thinks "it was only the Chinese woman and her daughter [of all the people in the restaurant] that I really envied. It was clear that they had something precious: something that I wanted badly. Something that I wanted to share in" (7). He travels back to Australia at Easter time of the same year, to reunite with his father and encourage him to reconcile with Roger Anstruther, and seeks out the Chinese woman and her daughter again. There is an oddly coincidental revelation about toothbrushes, and, as he tells the woman his story, she wisely observes: "This girl Poppy. . . . She interests me. Out of all the people you met on your journey, there is something very special about her. She was the one who understood you the best, I think" (219). At this point even the Chinese woman has realized what Poppy realized quickly, what the reader has *begun* to realize, and what Max will finally see: that he is homosexual and that Poppy intended to bring him together with her uncle Clive. Her invitation designed to set this up has failed because, typically, Max misread the clues, thinking she was trying to pair him off with her mother. A text from Clive ending with "X" has bewildered and discomfited him en route to Scotland. (An earlier hint of Max's confusion, one that links him curiously with Robert in *The House of Sleep,* comes when he comments, "I don't like to pee standing up" [14].)

A serenity comes over Max as he thinks of his need to talk to someone, discards his excuses, and phones Clive in London, reflecting that "the first thing I find attractive in someone, nine times out of ten, is his voice" (332); on the following page he tells the reader that his story is over, as "I telephoned Clive and knew that everything was going to be all right" (333).

Although Max's quest has reached its conclusion, the novel has not, and there is a final chapter, called "√ -1" which takes *Terrible Privacy* in a newly metafictional direction; on the beach Max encounters a family group, a husband and wife and two pale daughters; in conversation the man reveals that he has seen Max before, that he is a writer, mostly of novels, and that he is "Just finishing one, since you ask. Getting very close to the end now" (335). This is of course Jonathan Coe, who reveals the source of Max's story in his own experience—observing a Chinese woman and her daughter, mixing up a meeting in the Botanical Gardens because there are two tea rooms there, then his conversations with friends, his thoughts about a common household object (a toothbrush): "'So you see, what generally happens—to answer your original question—is that I get all sorts of different ideas, from all sorts of different places, and when I start putting them together, other things start to emerge. People, to be precise. Characters. Or in this particular instance'—he looked directly at me—'*you*'" (337). Further conversation further convinces Max of his contingent existence only in the author's imagination and that his story ends precisely because, and when, the author stops telling it.

One detail the Jonathan Coe figure shares with Max is how his friend "started telling me about these works by Tacita Dean that were inspired by the Donald Crowhurst story, and she also put me on to this brilliant book about him by Nicolas Tomalin and Ron Hall" (337).

Donald Crowhurst and his own tragic story of terrible privacy is one of the two very important referential nodes Coe uses in this novel. Crowhurst, a real yachtsman, is at the same time an object of interest to Max; a link to Clive, since he learns about Crowhurst by reading a letter from Clive to Poppy; and an analogue and structuring device. There are even local touches; Donald Crowhurst's mad speculations included discussing the square root of minus one and, as we have seen, that impossible mathematical proposition becomes the title of the last chapter of the book; perhaps it is meant to suggest the oddly involuted narrative, with its confusion of levels, in which the fictional character converses with his creator about the conditions of his creation and the limits of his action. This metaphysical or existential tangle is reminiscent of John Fowles's metafictional neo-Victorian novel *The French Lieutenant's Woman* (1969), in which the author boards a train carriage with his protagonist and ostentatiously flips a coin to decide which of two narrative endings to supply first. An even better linkage is with Flann O'Brien's *At Swim-Two-Birds* (1939), one of Coe's touchstone novels when he was beginning to write, in which fictional characters, liberated by their author's sleepiness, avenge themselves (for instance, he has raped one of his creations and fathered a child) by drugging him and beating him. Fowles puts the author alongside and in the same fictional plane as his characters; O'Brien goes further and grants the fictional characters authority over their own author. Coe's practice is more like Fowles's, but both books subvert the conventional separation of realms that keeps author and fictional characters apart, in the move that David Lodge calls "short circuit."[39]

As Clive writes, he became interested first in Sir Francis Chichester, who sailed around the world single-handed in 1968 and became a national hero. The *Sunday Times* then announced a prize for the yachtsman who completed the fastest single-handed *nonstop* navigation of the world (Chichester had stopped once, in Australia), and Donald Crowhurst was one of the entrants. It became clear that he was to round-the-world sailing roughly what Maxwell Sim is to toothbrush-selling or heterosexual seduction. Crowhurst's predicament arose from his decision, fairly soon, not to attempt to win but to sail aimlessly in an empty sea, falsifying his location and his movements. Finishing rather than quitting would avoid ruinous financial penalties, but finishing second or third rather than winning would avoid too much attention; to his dismay the sailors ahead of him dropped out and he was likely to finish first, attracting the kind of scrutiny that would expose his deception. This drove him mad, into work on the square root of minus one and speculation on the mutation of some people, including him, into "second generation cosmic beings" (62), into incoherent scrawls, and finally into suicide.

Why is this narrative so carefully supplied and linked in various ways to the story of Maxwell Sim? One hint is supplied by Clive's use of the term "the terrible privacy of his tiny cabin" (55), which looks forward to the terrible privacy of Max's lonely Prius. He later wonders how Crowhurst could have survived the "even more terrible privacy of family life?" (59)—another commentary that applies as well to Max. As Max nears the end of his own lonely voyage, he too becomes mad, he too gives way and, unlike Crowhurst, who wrote dementedly in a sailor's log, converses with "Emma," his onboard computerized GPS system, believing that she is replying to him. He recognizes the analogy, stripping off his clothes because Crowhurst was naked at the end; telling Emma that they are in the doldrums—like Crowhurst; declaring "I AM NOT MAXWELL SIM ANY MORE. I AM DONALD CROWHURST and I have to follow in his path and repeat his mistakes" (287); and thinking that he and Emma, a disembodied voice, are "like those 'cosmic beings' that Crowhurst thought everyone was going to turn into" (283)—a conclusion that leads him to propose marriage to her. There is even an entirely fortuitous, or factitious, link between Maxwell and Clive that runs through Sir Francis Chichester; Maxwell remembers watching the coverage of Chichester's homecoming with his mother the night that Roger Anstruther made his sole visit to their home.

Roger Anstruther is the key to the other important linkage outside the novel. In the first instance, it links *Terrible Privacy* to Coe's biography of B. S. Johnson, *Like A Fiery Elephant,* published in 2005. One hint comes in Max's deluded ramblings near the end of his voyage: "The terrible privacy, as Clive called it? I'm not surprised. Nobody could be expected to handle solitude like that, and why should you be any different? You're human like the rest of them" (285). This is a reference (unrecognized, of course, by Max) to B. S. Johnson's play *You're Human Like the Rest of Them,* written in 1964 and published in 1970. Its subject is a man confronting his own mortality.

In the Coda of *Like a Fiery Elephant,* Coe offers what he calls "*a* story about B. S. Johnson" (421), that is, a framework for interpretation of a number of mysterious actions in his life, entries in his writings, and even the events of the last few days of his life. He finds the secret in a certain Michael Bannard, who was Johnson's very close friend when they were young men; Johnson wrote obliquely about Bannard wanting him to go too far and linked the two of them to "the White Goddess," a mythic concept mostly identified with the work of Robert Graves. He traces appearances of Michael Bannard in Johnson's writing and, through some impressive sleuthing, discovers that at the very end of the author's life Bannard had probably appeared in public to heckle him; that Bannard was homosexual and in fact hated women and had perhaps invited Johnson to join him in that stance; that with his wife away, and in emotional crisis, Johnson had sought out Bannard on the night he killed himself. This leads on to a new way of interpreting Johnson's modernist ambitions and much else, but at this point it is important to note the tentative conclusions Coe draws: "we were in fact dealing with a very complicated friendship, something much more fraught than the simple love affair between two men which I had been started to construct in my mind. Why the talk of 'submission to MB'?" (434).

The "simple love affair between two men" may appear in *Terrible Privacy,* at least embryonically, in the final éclaircissement between Maxwell and Clive. But the relationship between Johnson and Bannard forms the substrate for the relationship, finally discovered by Max when he reads his father's account, called "The Rising Sun," of his own history with Roger Anstruther. Anstruther had dominated Mr. Sim from the beginning of their relationship, which began over a copy of *Four Quartets.* Anstruther, self-confident and culturally aware, "dominated me completely. It was a relationship which (at first) suited both of our needs perfectly" (251). Like Michael Bannard, Anstruther is ruthless toward his disciple; like him, he warns that "women are not to be trusted, or relied upon" (261); like him, he has some deep commitment to the White Goddess, explaining "'You should pay attention to this, Harold, if you're serious about wanting to write. The Goddess is where all poetic inspiration comes from. Read Robert Graves if you don't believe me. You'd better keep on the right side of her. Unfortunately . . .' (he put the book down and lay back on the grass, his head resting on folded hands) 'she absolutely disapproves of homosexuality, and has terrible punishments in store for those who practice it. Bad news for the likes of us'" (262).

In other words, Coe is fleshing out what he has intuited of Johnson's entanglement with Bannard, making explicit what is indirectly hinted in Johnson's poems and fictions and letters and the recollections of his friends. Roger Anstruther, who simultaneously fascinates and irritates Harold Sim by his outrageousness and his demands for submission, disapproves (naturally) of his new relationship with the secretary Barbara and offers to "rescue" him. Through a complicated misunderstanding—the two pubs called the Rising Sun at which Harold and Roger separately turn up, missing each other—the rescue miscarries, Barbara becomes pregnant, and Max is born. That Harold had already acknowledged "I could no longer tell myself lies about my own nature" (273) makes doubly pathetic his denial of it in a long marriage to Barbara, unhappy for both of them.

Discovering that Roger Anstruther, who wrote many postcards to Harold Sim, is in Australia leads Maxwell to try to bring them together. Their encounter fails, once again, in an uncanny repeat as each goes to the tea room at the Melbourne Botanical Gardens, only to discover that, just as there are two pubs called the Rising Sun, there are two tea rooms at the Melbourne Botanical Gardens.

The reunion, then, does not come off, in the pages of the novel, just as Maxwell's reunion with the Chinese woman fails to deliver what he is looking for, but in the case of father and son, there is at least a recognition of their true natures and a new and unprecedented understanding of his father by Maxwell. This constitutes a "happy" turn to their narratives, the sharpest divergence from the suicidal conclusion Johnson reached.

Although intricate plotting and intertextual connection to disparate texts outside the novel are common features in Coe's work, the combination of those features with a central character of uncommon lack of perception is a new development in *Terrible Privacy,* and one that received some unusually negative reactions from reviewers. Alex Clark's summary is one of the strongest demurrals: "Jonathan Coe's ninth novel is such a sprawling mess of a book, a hodge-podge of picaresque plotting, shifting modes and voices, postmodern intervention and questionably humorous social observation that it comes as a relief when his narrator addresses us directly, near the novel's close, with the words: It's been a long haul, I know. Thanks to all the people who have stayed with me. Really, I appreciate it. And I admire your stamina, I must say. Most impressive" (6).

Chris Barton in the *Los Angeles Times* indicted the book for feeling "overwritten to the point of stretching plausibility"—although one might say it is hardly aiming at any sort of strict verisimilitude. Kathleen Byrne acknowledged the importance of Coe's theme of solitariness but continued, "then we are up against Coe's method of telling, troublesome in itself with its four interwoven narratives involving Sim's father as a young man in bohemian London, two separate-although-disastrous-in-their-own-way family vacations, and the real-life tale of amateur yachtsman Donald Crowhurst, who disappeared at sea in 1969" (R4). Stefan Beck criticizes the author for "heavy-handed contrivances."[40] And William Giraldi similarly objects to what he considers tonal inconsistencies: "All along, 'The Terrible Privacy of Maxwell Sim' yearns to unfurl into a theater of absurdity: on top of the G.P.S. voice with sex appeal, a stranger dies on a plane while listening to Max's story, and a mugger asks him for directions after the mugging. Coe's publishers bill the book as a 'satire and modern-day picaresque,' but they must have another novel in mind because this one is by turns much too sincere and much too silly and, in the end, much too somber. Satire cannot accommodate soul-crushing sadness, and little in life can be sadder than the line Max imagines for his gravestone: 'Here lies Maxwell Sim, the most unnecessary person ever born.'"

In defense of the novel one may say, of course, that there is no accounting for tastes but also, more significant, that the subtext of most of these objections is *impatience.* A more patient reading, a slower reading of the novel brings out the deep humanity in the story of a nobody and justifies the "contrivances" required to link him to his father, to Donald Crowhurst, and to B. S. Johnson.

A particular point of disagreement is the ending. Coe admits that his editors objected to the ending, and "many readers agreed with their assessment" when the book was published in England.[41] One who objected—initially—was Ed Park, in a thorough and mixed review of the book. He writes, "As in *Like a Fiery Elephant,* Coe reserves the most brain-scrambling shock for the very end. The brief final section of *Maxwell Sim,* which features an appearance by Coe himself, at first irritated me—the sort of cute postmodern touch that seemed hardly simpati-Coe. On a second read, though, it became chillingly brilliant. The coda violates Max's privacy in a way that goes beyond simple plot and completes a starting transformation, albeit not the alchemical one that's been lurking." Coe's reflection on such irritation, even anger, is shock, but he concludes, "I'm sort of reconciled now to the idea that I won't please everybody, . . . but by walking those two simultaneous paths"—between populism and modernist or postmodernist literary fiction—"I run the risk of not pleasing anybody at all."[42]

Perhaps what he has found, although he might not welcome this suggestion, is a "Third Way." Clive uses this term to identify Donald Crowhurst's "solution" to his problem, when neither quitting nor permitting himself to win will work, and (in one of the few political passages of the novel) he calls it "a solution worthy, you might say, of our very own Prime Minister: For—just like Mr. Blair, faced with the twin undesirables of free market capitalism and state-heavy socialism," Crowhurst found a Third Way. And—perhaps this also applies to Coe—"it was, even his critics would have to admit, an extremely daring and ingenious one" (56).

Coe's 2013 novel *Expo 58* is less intricate, less playful, than *The Terrible Privacy of Maxwell Sim;* it is also more comic, although the comedy is, as usual, tinged with sadness. And, although it would be wrong to try to force it into the condition-of-England frame—if only because more than half of it is set in Belgium—nevertheless it somewhat resembles Coe's earlier books *What a Carve Up!, The Rotters' Club,* and *The Closed Circle* in representing a decade. Not the entire decade, of course, in part because it does not begin until 1958, but there is much detail about what life was like in the 1950s. Some of this is used for comedy, as when everybody smokes cigarettes all the time (some even suggesting that smoking during pregnancy is a particularly good idea) or people wonder what one calls rock and roll, or marvel at the new Continental bed furnishings called the duvet, or discuss the new novelist of international espionage, Ian Fleming. Other elements, including controversy about whether Britain should be thought of as part of Europe or whether the proper role of the foreign service is to promote British business or the Cold War competition between the United States and the Soviet Union, are more important and more lasting. As this list of topics suggest, the novel continues Coe's successful practice of foregrounding an individual story that ramifies outward in political and sociological directions. At the center is Thomas Foley, a "little man" caught up in phenomena he hardly understands. But the phenomena themselves, ranging from international espionage to choices about marriage, are equally explored.

One more feature connects *Expo 58* to Coe's earlier oeuvre: "Thomas's ears always pricked up when he heard Beatrix's name. She was by some way the most interesting (and least respectable) member of Sylvia's family, a compulsive romantic adventuress rarely held back by the fact that she had an infant daughter to look after. The pleasure of tutting over the latest Beatrix scandal was one of the few that Thomas and Sylvia could share together: from both of them, her exploits provoked routine outbursts of disapproval and secret pangs of envy in equal measure.[43] The news that this Beatrix has broken her neck in a car accident clinches her identity with the Beatrix who, in *The Rain Before It Falls,* proves such a disastrous mother to Thea (and grandmother to Imogen) as well as a treacherous and exploitative cousin to Rosamond. And Gill, Thomas Foley's daughter, an infant at the time of narration, is, then, the Gill who attends to Rosamond's funeral and the disposition of her effects and listens to the tapes with her *own* daughters.

The novel's title refers to the Exposition Universelle et Internationale de Bruxelles 1958, mounted for several purposes, of which the "final aim" was "to contribute to the development of a genuine unity of mankind, based upon respect for human personality" (2). Coe needs no special effort to highlight the ironies of that aim for readers who know what has happened in the fifty-five years since. Peter Carty, alluding to the "fleeting utopian vision" of the Expo, calls it "an event that was simultaneously surreal and willfully Postmodern."[44] Designed to be internationalist, to smooth over national differences, it also inexorably invited participating countries to a display of nationalism. The British pavilion was designed to show off advances in nuclear technology (withdrawn because they do not work) and to display the best of British (one mischievous suggestion that toilets and sanitary engineering should have pride of place is shouted down). One reviewer identified the novel's main questions as "what is Britishness and how can it be summed up?"[45] Coe seems to concur, as he explained in an interview conducted in France:

> Periodically, we have these debates in the UK about what is Britishness, what is Englishness. When I was writing the book in 2012 we were putting on the Olympics and Danny Boyle did a magnificent Olympic opening ceremony which asked exactly those questions. It's a topic that comes up occasionally in the UK but when I come abroad and talk to journalists in Belgium, France and Italy about my books, they always perceive these books as being very English. When I ask them what that means they're

> never able to tell me. And when they ask me what I think it means I'm never able to tell them. There's definitely something about Englishness and the English sense of humour which seems to fascinate our continental allies.[46]

Thomas's involvement in the events of this novel comes about rather randomly. He is a midlevel bureaucrat at the Central Office of Information who is chosen to supervise the Brittannia, a pub installed in the British pavilion at the Brussels Exposition to foreground the "best of British." Someone has discovered that Thomas's father was a publican and that his mother was Belgian. He has in fact spent some time working in a pub, and it turns out that there is very little administration involved in the Brittannia; instead, he is a cat's-paw in intrigues involving the British, American, and Soviet intelligence agencies. Having been assigned to the Brussels pavilion, Thomas is immediately accosted by two men who appear as if from nowhere and introduce themselves as Mr. Wayne and Mr. Radford. After promising to drive him home and giving him a long, obvious, and funny cross-examination, they leave him miles from home. He has been recruited as a spy, without his consent or even awareness.

Although the espionage plot becomes much more sober as the novel draws to its conclusion, it is played largely for comedy. The quality of the conversation between the two spymasters, which seems based in traditional British musical hall comedy, appears in a passage like this one:

> "Ah, yes. The Classics. Nothing like a bit of classical music, is there? I expect you like Tchaikovsky?"
> "Of course. Who doesn't?"
> "What about the more modern bods? Stravinsky, say?"
> "Oh, yes. First rate."
> "Shostakovich?"
> "Haven't heard much."
> "Prokofiev?" (37)

Having named all the Russian composers they can think of in search of Communist proclivities, they turn to literature and question him about Dostoevsky and Tolstoy; then, turning to a clumsy effort to find out if he is homosexual, one of them (their speeches are seldom tagged, making them even more indistinguishable) mentions the "gentleman's toilet at Hyde Park Corner," segueing quickly to "Ghastly. Do you know it?" (38). Mr. Radford and Mr. Wayne reappear from time to time, including in Brussels, where they assign Thomas to go out with a young American woman about whom they have suspicions; they also, somewhat mischievously, suggest that his wife, Sylvia, is having an affair with the neighbor while her husband is away.

Near the end of the novel, when the seriousness of these two apparently incompetent operatives becomes much clearer, Coe increases the silliness of their dialogue. They identify the barmaid at the Brittania as having been a Soviet agent.

> He gaped back at them. "The barmaid? Surely not!"
> "Yes—Shirley Knott. Precisely."
> "You've got it in one, old boy." (242)

The secrets are being passed from Shirley Knott to a Soviet spy in the sachet of salt provided with bags of crisps (this is related as one of the miracle inventions of the 1950s). Emily, a supposedly naïve girl from Wisconsin but actually an American spy, figures it out:

> "Mr Chersky had the sachet."
> "He had the sachet and the packet."
> "He had the sachet and the packet in his pocket."
> "He had the sachet and the packet in the pocket of his jacket." (244)

The French reviewer Alexis Liebaert called it "un roman d'espionnage hautement comique—peut-être le plus hilarant de son auteur."[47] Lucy Kellaway saw the qualification of that hilarity and called it "Coe at his funny-serious best, offering his idiosyncratic mixture of slapstick and profundity."[48] The mixture of elements did not please everybody, as James Lasdun complained: "What to make of all this? The final effect is extremely hard to define. It is too self-conscious to pass as a straight period piece. Too gracefully written and carefully constructed to read as throwaway spoof or parody. Too madcap to take very seriously. 'Homage' perhaps best describes its essentially affectionate relationship to the materials it draws on, but that isn't quite it either."[49]

What does the author say about *Expo 58*? "My latest novel can be read in a number of ways: as a traditional English 'comic novel' in the tradition of Henry Fielding, Michael Frayn and Kingsley Amis; as an *hommage* to British comedy films of the 1930s, 40s and 50s; as a parody of Cold War spy fiction; and as the latest chapter in an interlocking network of novels and short stories which I have been writing for the past two decades."[50]

The story of Thomas's unwilling and mostly uncomprehending work as an agent is linked to his dissatisfaction with his marriage; low key at first, it develops as he stays in Brussels and seems to lose interest in his wife and daughter under the impact of "Europe," quasi-bachelorhood, and an attractive and willing Belgian hostess named Anneke. The letters the two Foleys, man and wife, exchange are marvelously constructed by Coe. Thomas is secretive and then defensive about the women in Brussels; Sylvia is jealous and perhaps for this reason may hint at more to the relationship with neighbor Mr. Sparks than actually exists. (It is true that he takes her to restaurant meals and films, something, it is suggested, that her husband does not do.) And Foley's readiness to suspect an affair is plausibly explained further by projection; guilty of pretending to be unmarried and of flirting and eventually sleeping with another woman, he finds it in his psychological interest to believe he is the offended party. The "evidence" comes in the form of a "corn cushion" he finds in his bed: Sparks is famously a martyr to corns. A choral comment on Thomas's marriage is supplied by his Belgian mother, whose knowledge of marital unhappiness strengthens her pleas to Thomas to treat his wife properly. Aware of his infidelity with Anneke, she tells her son, "I'm telling you right now: forget all about her. She's not important. Your wife is important. Your family is important. Of course you feel unhappy now. That's because you've been stupid. But that will change. The feeling will pass" (232).

Thomas does write to Anneke, breaking off the relationship, but he probably had little choice, as in his final conversation with Wayne and Radford he learns that they have compromising photographs of his night with Anneke, taken through a skylight, photographs they use to blackmail him into continuing to inform, at this point in his new job at an engineering firm. Thomas's final reflections on his involvement with Radford, Wayne, Anneke, and Brussels are melancholy ones:

> Much later (many years later, in fact) he would find himself wondering why he had agreed to their terms, why he had let himself be cornered so easily. It would have been simpler, quicker and cleaner to tell them both to go to hell. Was his marriage really worth saving at such a high price? Because the thing that struck him as most mysterious about his adventures at Expo 58 was not, after all, the improbable intrigue in which he had become embroiled, but the proven fragility of his loyalty to Sylvia during those weeks. As he grew older, it seemed to him more and more likely that he had done a cruel thing, not by marrying her, but by staying married to her. That was the real pity of it: that he had condemned her, through vacillation, to a life of unrest. (250)

The closing reflection links Thomas Foley to Maxwell Sim's father, who condemned a woman to an unhappy lifetime by marrying her, and to a panoply of Jonathan Coe's male protagonists, who usually fail to do the daring thing, be it following up opportunities with women or freeing themselves from the lineaments of their ordinary lives.

By contrast with Coe's earlier novels *What a Carve Up!* and *The House of Sleep*, *Expo 58* is more unitary, less invested in bricolage and intertextuality. Readers would have no cause to object to it, as Alex Clark did to *Terrible Privacy*, on the grounds of "postmodern intervention." The only deviation from more or less straightforward third-person narration is the inclusion in the chapter called "The girl from Wisconsin" of seven letters exchanged by Thomas and Sylvia Foley. These are brilliantly composed as a series of half-defensive moves in a passive-aggressive contest. Having allowed a week to pass before writing, Thomas must exaggerate how busy and important he is. Sylvia replies with a letter that makes clear she resents not being invited to Brussels, making a barbed observation that Thomas has not mentioned their daughter and declaring that Mr. Sparks "has been most obliging since you went away" (105)—performing household tasks that her husband had left unfinished. In his next letter Thomas escalates by mentioning Anneke, "his guardian angel" (106); when Sylvia responds with more laudatory news of Norman (no longer "Mr. Sparks"), his next letter includes the observation that "I had not got him down as the sort of chap who was good at babies, but now that I think of it, I suppose there is something oddly feminine about him, so it probably makes a kind of sense" (109). Here he mentions both Anneke and Emily, the American girl. Sylvia's reaction is "I'm sure that you, he [a friend called Tony], Emily and Anneke must make a most appealing foursome when you all go out together to sample the bright lights of an evening. Back here, alas, I have nothing so glamorous to distract me" (112)—aside from dinner and the flicks with Norman. The last from Thomas Foley mentions the Russian's passion for Smith's Salt and Shake crisps, with their salt sachets, and concludes with a P.S.: "So, no diminution in the attentions of Mr. Sparks, I see. A trip to the pictures, and dinner afterwards! It's a good job I'm not the jealous type" (115). Each of these letters is a sort of masterpiece of feline indirection, self-protective silence, and innuendo.

There are some important intertextual relationships, beyond the one to *The Rain Before It Falls.* The lesser one, perhaps, is triggered when the Director of Exhibitions of the Central Office of Information calls Thomas "our man in Brussels" (11). This echoes the title of Graham Greene's *Our Man in Havana* (published in 1958, the year in which Coe's book is set), a novel that treats espionage comically. Havana under dictator Fulgencio Batista was undoubtedly a more exotic and dangerous locale for a spy's posting than Brussels (Belgium is often treated as inherently comic in British culture), but Greene's protagonist is, like Foley, inducted into MI6, the British overseas intelligence service, despite his lack of qualifications—he is a vacuum-cleaner salesman—and, although he is deliberately pretending to perform espionage tasks whereas Foley is doing so only inadvertently or as an unwitting diversion from the real spying, the novels share a darkly comic approach to espionage. Robert McCrum insists that "with the exception of Graham Greene in *Our Man in Havana*, no one has managed to marry these genres"—the thriller and the comedy. "But *Expo 58* is quite the equal of Green's 'entertainment.'"[51]

The other, stronger intertextuality links to Ian Fleming's James Bond novels. Thomas finds himself reading one of them, *From Russia with Love,* after Mr. Radford and Mr. Wayne mention them. Having read a bit and wondering about how Fleming knew so much about espionage, he puts himself into the Bond context: "it was pretty flattering, after all, that someone should want to cast him as the bait in a romantic mousetrap [later he learns that he was more like a distraction from the real action]. If they really saw him as that sort of fellow—the irresistible romantic hero type—who was he to argue? . . . Thomas had been more than dimly conscious, these last two days, of a certain heroic glow at the thought that he was stepping up to the wicket now that his name had been called, and doing his bit for Queen and country" (151).

Earlier Radford and Wayne had complained that reading the Bond books was having a bad effect on their department, and they follow with a typical passage of stichomythia:

> "I mean, dash it all, Radford, when was the last time you did that?"
> "Bump somebody off, you mean?"
> "No—sleep with a different woman."
> "Well, depends what you mean. Different from whom?"
> "Different from the last one you slept with, I suppose."
> "Oh, well, in that case, I couldn't possibly say."
> "Within living memory?"
> "Hardly, old boy."
> "Well, there you are, then. Not the smallest basis of reality in it"
> (140–141)

Thomas, as it turns out, if not very successful in crafty espionage, is a bit more so in sleeping with a different woman. Otherwise, as Cressida Connolly insists, he is "a sort of anti-James Bond. He lives in Tooting with a young wife and baby daughter, next door to a stock comic character who suffers terribly from corns. It is likely that he has never tasted a Martini, nor even an olive."[52]

He is not quite so Pooterish as Maxwell Sim—for one thing, he is strikingly handsome and attractive to women—but his suburban limitations make him another of the protagonists in whom Coe has specialized, ordinary men, men who in some ways are unlikeable to readers but whom the reader ends up caring about.

Also in 2013, Coe published *The Story of Gulliver,* a retelling of Jonathan Swift's eighteenth-century classic. (One interviewer suggested that *Gulliver's Travels* might be one model for the plot of *Expo 58,* with its travel motif and its gullible hero. That he worked on the two books simultaneously might have led to some interpenetration.) This was Coe's part in a "new publishing drive for children" called "Save the Story," in which classic tales are retold by leading novelists in a way that is described as "fresh, idiosyncratic and winning."[53] Kate Kellaway writes that *The Story of Gulliver* "has Jonathan Coe's hallmark clarity. The style is attractive, entertaining, non-exclamatory (Swift would have approved)." Given his dedication to strong plotting in contemporary fiction, often defended, a natural cause for his support is to "Save the Story."

Conclusion

Looking back over the ten novels that constitute Jonathan Coe's major work so far—though not ignoring his biographies, literary journalism, and musical work—how ought one to characterize it? Among the generalizations sometimes applied to his work, none is sufficiently encompassing. Prince of postmodernism? Perhaps that applies to the writer of *The House of Sleep* and *What a Carve Up!* and, in a different way, *The Terrible Privacy of Maxwell Sim*. But what about *The Rain Before It Falls?* Or *Expo 58?*

A fiery political novelist? That certainly accounts for the energy of *What a Carve Up!, The Rotters' Club,* and *The Closed Circle,* but much less for some other books: *The Rain Before It Falls,* for instance, is almost devoid of political comment. The author of broad-canvas, panoramic novels with multiple "main" characters? Again, *The Rotters' Club, Closed Circle,* and *What a Carve Up!*—but hardly applicable to *A Touch of Love, An Accidental Woman, The Rain Before It Falls,* or *The Terrible Privacy of Maxwell Sim.*

What this suggests, and what Coe himself has acknowledged, is that, for many commentators, a Jonathan Coe novel is *What a Carve Up!* or at least something similar to it, and, to the extent that his later—or, for that matter, earlier—books fail to conform to its pattern, they are anomalies or disappointments. This is despite the great diversity and multifariousness of his output, which would show to a careful examiner that *What a Carve Up!* is not the template for most of his other books.

As Coe said ruefully, "It's become a matter of honour for most reviewers in this country (and many readers) to remind me as often as possible that *What a Carve Up!* is my best novel. No middle-aged novelist who is still trying to make a living from writing likes to be told that his last five books are not a patch on the one he wrote when he was in his early 30s, but I suppose I'm obliged to entertain the idea that there might be something in it."[1]

Considering him "the author of *What a Carve Up!*" is, in a sense, unfair; as he points out, he was by the time of this interview the author of five more recent novels, and another followed them in 2013. *What a Carve Up!*, then, is one of his *early* novels. And yet, looked at another way, even if it is unjust, this view is a tribute to the lasting and almost universally accepted magisterial quality of that breakthrough book. One thinks of Gustave Flaubert as the author of *Madame Bovary,* although he wrote more books after it than before it; Thackeray as the author of *Vanity Fair;* Charlotte Bronte as the author of *Jane Eyre.* While possibly "unfair" to these novelists' later work, such a recognition (the better part of two centuries after any of these texts appeared) is also a tribute. *What a Carve Up!* is not *Madame Bovary,* as Jonathan Coe undoubtedly would point out. But if his lasting reputation should turn out to be as "the author of *What a Carve Up!*," that is no mean feat.

Nevertheless is it is important to recognize the breadth of his work, the originality and the willingness to swerve off in new directions, particularly in the three books that have followed *The Closed Circle.* If one thinks of his ten-book career as a sort of triptych, the central (and arguably largest) panel consists of *What a Carve Up!* and *The House of Sleep, The Rotters' Club* and *The Closed Circle.* On the left are the three early novels, undervalued at the time of publication: *An Accidental Woman, A Touch of Love,* and *The Dwarves of Death.* The right panel features *The Rain Before It Falls, The Terrible Privacy of Maxwell Sim,* and *Expo 58.*

There are some generalizing, or summative, comments that may help to see Coe's oeuvre as a whole. As we have seen, he is versatile, imaginative, eager to move in a new direction, and, in that respect, daring.

Nick Rennison commented on "his ability to combine formal daring with the tradition of English comic fiction which goes back through Kingsley Amis to Evelyn Waugh."[2] The balance of comedy with formal daring shifts from one book to another, both reaching their apogee in, yes, *What a Carve Up!* There is more comedy in *Expo 58* than *Terrible Privacy* but less formal daring, and so on.

Aside from these qualities, one might apply to Jonathan Coe's fiction the comment he made in trying to explain to an interviewer why his books are popular in France: "I can only go on what I'm told by French journalists: that they feel rather starved of novels which feature strong narratives, humour, and engagement with contemporary social issues."[3]

To that very apt account one might add his continuing, lively, and meaningful interest in other genres. Coe has said that being a novelist was his third choice of career, after performing as a musician and directing films. Readers can be happy that he became a writer but will also notice the way that music and film informs his fiction—either comically, as in Terry's interest in the Italian neorealist director Salvatore Ortese and his classics "*Il Costo della Pesca* (*Dearly*

Have We Paid for the Mullet, 1947)" and "the more upbeat *Morte da Fame* (*Death from Starvation,* 1955)"[4]—or more structurally, as in the use of the movie *What a Carve Up!* as plot device, source of Michael Owen's lifelong obsession, and symbolic referent. Likewise, although music is never just background, it ranges from a minor element in *The House of Sleep* to a major thematic device in *The Rain Before It Falls* to the very substance of the main character's life in *The Dwarves of Death* and its short sequel, "9th and 13th."

Finally, there is Coe's frequent and clever use of borrowed material. In one of the books that constituted an early influence, Flann O'Brien's *At Swim-Two-Birds,* the narrator explains, "The modern novel should be largely a work of reference. Most authors spend their time saying what has been said before—usually said much better. A wealth of references to existing works would acquaint the reader instantaneously with the nature of each character, would obviate tiresome explanations and would effectively preclude mountebanks, upstarts, thimbleriggers and persons of inferior education from an understanding of contemporary literature."[5] Even O'Brien is only partly serious (the addressee of this manifesto replies, "That is all my bum"), and Coe will never go so far. But he is a writer astutely aware of his influences, resourceful in using them, and generous in acknowledging them. The best examples are probably the use of B. S. Johnson in *The Terrible Privacy of Maxwell Sim* and the *hommage* to Rosamond Lehmann in *The Rain Before It Falls,* but even the inclusion of Simone Weil's *Gravity and Grace* in *A Touch of Love* and *The House of Sleep* is an important intertextual reference. Coe is influenced, but his influences produce no anxiety.

Jonathan Coe has carved out a special niche in the modern British literary novel. His books are popular, both in his home country and even more on the Continent, and yet are acknowledged by critics as "literary" rather than "popular" fiction. They feature complex plots, often built upon generous use of coincidence, and they insist on humor. He has managed to bridge the popular/literary divide, to please many readers, and to please them with some of the traditional pleasures of reading fiction—plotting, comedy—while continuing to enjoy the status that led to multiweek treatment by Professor John Mullan in the *Guardian* series on the art of fiction. Nick Hornby, who is not just a popular novelist but also a sort of culture warrior against the preciousness of the literary novel, writes about the "kind of writing [that] tends to be admired by critics more than by book buyers, if the best-seller lists can be admitted as evidence," and goes on to decry the boredom of much "literary fiction" and the idea that "books should be hard work, and that unless they're hard work, they're not doing us any good."[6] This same enemy of the excesses of "literary fiction" praises Coe (reviewing *Like a Fiery Elephant)* for being "imaginative and interrogative about the form and shape of the book" and acknowledges him, in a tribute that will serve very well as a summary judgment, as "probably the best English novelist of his generation."[7]

NOTES

ONE: Understanding Jonathan Coe

1. Nick Hornby, *The Polysyllabic Spree* (San Francisco: Believer Books, 2004), 108.
2. Florence Noiville, "The Contemporary British Novel—A French Perspective," *European Journal of English Studies* 10 (December 2006), 298.
3. Steven Zeitchik, "The Best Writer You've Never Heard Of," *Publisher's Weekly,* September 5, 2005, 22.
4. Robert Hanks, "Modern Life's a Rotten Disappointment," *Independent,* October 8, 2004, 35.
5. Richard Eder, "The House of Sleep," *Los Angeles Times,* March 1, 1998.
6. Jonathan Coe, "Low Culture Rises above Its Critics," *Sunday Times,* November 20, 1994.
7. Terry Grimley, "A Bestseller Straight from 70s Brum," *Birmingham Post,* March 14, 2001, 13.
8. Jonathan Coe, *The Rotters' Club* (London: Viking, 2001), 135.
9. Philip Tew, "Johanthan Coe," in *Writers Talk: Conversations with Contemporary British Novelists,* ed. Philip Tew, Fiona Tolan, and Leigh Wilson (London: Continuum, 2008), 37.
10. Tom Lappin, "Waiting for Tony," *Scotland on Sunday,* August 17, 1997, Spectrum 11.
11. Sally Vincent, "A Bit of a Rotter," *Guardian Weekend,* February 23, 2001, 36.
12. Paul Laity, "A Life in Writing: Jonathan Coe," *Guardian,* May 28, 2010: 12; William May, "Closing the Circle: An Interview with Jonathan Coe," *From Self to Shelf: The Artist under Construction,* ed. Sally Bayley and William May (Newcastle: Cambridge Scholars, 2007), 70.
13. Grimley, "A Bestseller," 13.
14. Zeitchick, "The Best Writer You've Never Heard Of," 21.
15. Robert Winder, "A One-Man Avant-Garde," *New Statesman,* June 21, 2004.
16. Jonathan Coe, "My Literary Love Affair," *Guardian,* October 5, 2007, Review 4.
17. Robert Lichtig, "Pictures of You," *New Statesman,* September 20, 2007.
18. Jonathan Coe, "*The Terrible Privacy of Maxwell Sim,*" *Jonathan Coe—Writer,* http://www.jonathancoewriter.com/books/maxwellSim.html.
19. Mark Sanderson, "Mark Sanderson Finds an Unexceptional Man's Sad Life Both Compelling and Funny," *Daily Telegraph,* May 30, 2010, 30.
20. Jonathan Coe, *Expo 58* (London: Viking, 2013), 1.

TWO: Early Novels

1. Philip Tew, "Jonathan Coe," *Writers Talk: Conversations with Contemporary British Novelists,* ed. Philip Tew, Fiona Tolan, and Leigh Wilson (London: Continuum, 2008), 36.
2. B. S. Johnson, *Christie Malry's Own Double-Entry* (New York: New Directions, 2009), 165.
3. Tew, "Jonathan Coe," 37.
4. Lidia Vianu, "The Accidental Theme: Jonathan Coe, *The Accidental Woman,*" *Philologica Jassyensia* 4 (2008), 147.
5. Jonathan Coe, *The Accidental Woman* (London: Penguin, 2000), 4, 14.
6. Patricia Waugh, *Metafiction: The Theory and Practice of Self-Conscious Fiction* (London: Methuen, 1984), 2.
7. Johnson, *Christie Malry's Own Double-Entry,*147, 12.
8. Henry Fielding, *The Adventures of Joseph Andrews* (London: Oxford University Press, 1961), 375–76.
9. Tew, "Jonathan Coe," 37.
10. Jonathan Coe, *A Touch of Love* (London: Penguin, 1989), 35
11. Johnson, *Christie Malry's Own Double-Entry,*165.
12. JonathanCoe,"WritingtheContemporary," *Jonathancowriter.com,*http://www.jonathancoewriter.com/.
13. Coe, "Writing the Contemporary."
14. John Lanchester, "Strong Meat," *London Review of Books,* January 11, 1990, 11.
15. Bruno Portesi, "Confusion des sentiments," Parutions.com, October 22, 2004.
16. Jonathan Coe, *The Dwarves of Death* (London: Penguin, 1990), 22, 211.
17. Pamela Thurschwell, "Genre, Repetition and History in Jonathan Coe," *British Fiction Today,* ed. Philip Tew and Rod Mengham (London: Continuum, 2006), 37.
18. Christina Koning, "Anything but the Girl," *Guardian,* May 17, 1990.
19. Jennifer Potter, "Paisley Pattern Plot: 'The Dwarves of Death,'" *Independent,* May 27, 1990, 19.
20. Julian Symons, "Deep Down," *London Review of Books,* June 28, 1990, 21.
21. Corinne Le Dour-Zana, "Jonathan Coe fait ses gammes," *Plume Noir,* www.plume-noir.com/culture/livres/lesnainsetlamort.html.
22. William May, "Closing the Circle: An Interview with Jonathan Coe," *From Self to Shelf: The Artist under Construction,* ed. Sally Bayley and William May (Newcastle: Cambridge Scholars, 2007), 71.

THREE: Short Fiction and Nonfiction

1. Francois Gallix and Vanessa Guignery, "Jonathan Coe," *Novelists in the New Millennium: Conversations with Writers,* ed. Vanessa Guignery (London: Palgrave Macmillan, 2013), 38.
2. Jonathan Coe, *9th & 13th* (London: Penguin, 2005), 1.

3. Jonathan Coe, "The Madness of King George: Power Mad," *Film/Literature/Heritage: A Sight and Sound Reader,* ed. Ginette Vincenteau (London: British Film Institute, 2001), 135–138.
4. Jonathan Coe, "Hammer's Cosy Violence," *Sight and Sound* 6 (August 1996), 10–11.
5. "Jonathan Coe," *Mortification: Writers' Stories of Their Public Shame,* ed. Robin Robertson (New York: Fourth Estate, 2003), 148–149.
6. William May, "Closing the Circle: An Interview with Jonathan Coe," *From Self to Shelf: The Artist under Construction,* ed. Sally Bayley and William May (Newcastle: Cambridge Scholars, 2007), 70.
7. Cyril Connolly, *Enemies of Promise* (New York: Persea Books, 1983), 94.
8. Jonathan Coe, "What's So Funny about the British?" *The Times,* October 3, 2009, 42–43.
9. Jonathan Coe, "Low Culture Rises above Its Critics," *Sunday Times,* November 20, 1994.
10. Jonathan Coe, "'Great Spunky Unflincher': Laurence Sterne, B S Johnson and Me," *Shandean* 15 (2004), 19.
11. Jonathan Coe, introduction to B. S. Johnson, *The Unfortunates* (London: Picador, 1999), v–xv.
12. Jonathan Coe, preface to B. S. Johnson, *Well Done God!,* ed. Jonathan Coe, Philip Tew, and Julia Jordan (London: Picador, 2013), xi–xiv.
13. Jonathan Coe, introduction to Rosamond Lehmann, *Dusty Answer* (London: Flamingo, 1996), n.p.
14. Jonathan Coe, introduction to Rosamond Lehmann, *The Echoing Grove* (London: Virago, 2000), n.p.
15. Shirley Eaton, *Golden Girl* (London: B. T. Batsford, 1999), 98.
16. Gallix and Guignery, "Jonathan Coe," 40.
17. Jonathan Coe, *Humphrey Bogart: Take It and Like It* (New York: Grove Weidenfeld, 1991), 11.
18. Jonathan Coe, *Jimmy Stewart: A Wonderful Life* (New York: Arcade Publishing, 1994), 9.
19. Gallix and Guignery, "Jonathan Coe," 40–41.
20. Jonathan Coe, *Like a Fiery Elephant: The Story of B. S. Johnson* (New York: Continuum, 2004), 31.
21. Gallix and Guignery, "Jonathan Coe," 42.
22. Julian Evans, "Modernism's Suicide," *Prospect,* May 27, 2004; Anthony Thwaite, "A Novelist, but Not So Novel," *Sunday Telegraph,* June 6, 2004, 13; Robert Winder, "A One-man Avant-garde,' *New Statesman,* June 21, 2004, 49.
23. Rachel Cooke, "The Man Who Hated Stories," *Observer,* May 29, 2004, 14; Frank Kermode, "Retripotent," *London Review of Books,* August 5, 2004, 13.
24. Quoted in Arifa Akbar, "Coe's 'Experimental' Biography Wins £30,000 Prize," *Independent,* June 15, 2005, 8.
25. B. S. Johnson, *Christie Malry's Own Double-Entry* (New York: New Directions, 2009), 166.

FOUR: Breakthrough

1. Jonathan Coe, "Guardian Book Club: Week Three: Jonathan Coe on Writing What a Carve Up!" *Guardian,* April 16, 2011, review pages, 6.
2. Nick Hornby, *The Polysyllabic Spree* (San Francisco: Believer Books, 2004), 108; Willam Giraldi, "The Man Who Fell in Love with His G.P.S.," *New York Times Sunday Book Review,* April 10, 2011, BR8.
3. Coe, "Guardian Book Club," 6.
4. Jonathan Coe, "Author, Author: Aiming at a Beast called 'Thatcherism,'" *Guardian,* April 10, 2009, 15.
5. Coe, "Author, Author," 15.
6. Jonathan Coe, *What a Carve Up!* (London: Penguin, 1994), 76, 73.
7. Coe, "Author, Author," 15.
8. Dominic Head, *The Cambridge Introduction to Modern British Fiction, 1950–2000* (Cambridge: Cambridge University Press, 2002), 36.
9. Anthony Quinn, "Clawing, Brutish Gargoyles," *Independent,* April 23, 1994, 26.
10. Terry Eagleton, "Theydunnit," *London Review of Books,* April 28, 1994: 12.
11. Ryan Trimm, "Carving Up Value: The Tragicomic Thatcher Years in Jonathan Coe," *Thatcher & After: Margaret Thatcher and Her Afterlife in Contemporary Culture,* ed. Louisa Hadley and Elizabeth Ho (Basingstroke, Hants: Palgrave Macmillan, 2010), 173.
12. Richard Bradford, *The Novel Now: Contemporary British Fiction* (Oxford: Blackwell, 2007: 40.
13. Henry Sutton, "Life Beyond Hampstead: Gritty, Politically Engaged Novels Are Rare These Days," *Independent on Sunday,* November 2, 2003, 16.
14. William May, "Closing the Circle: An Interview with Jonathan Coe," *From Self to Shelf: The Artist under Construction,* ed. Sally Bayley and William May (Newcastle: Cambridge Scholars, 2007), 68.
15. Nicola Allen, *Marginality in the Contemporary British Novel* (London: Continuum, 2008), 23.
16. Dominic Head, "The Demise of Class Fiction," *A Concise Companion to Contemporary British Fiction,* ed. James F. English (Oxford: Blackwell, 2006), 243.
17. Jonathan Driscoll, *Evading Class in Contemporary British Literature* (London: Palgrave Macmillan, 2009), 157.
18. James Delingpole, "Third Person Second Nature," *Daily Telegraph,* February 24, 2001, 7.
19. James Delingpole, "Laying It On a Bit Thick," *Spectator,* April 14, 2001, 34.
20. Head, *Cambridge Introduction,* 47.
21. Hugh Barnes, "Carry on up the Comic Culture," *The Independent,* April 24, 1994, 33; Joel Yanofsky, "Comic Novel Has Message about '80s," *Gazette*(Montreal), March 18, 1995, H2.
22. Pamela Thurschwell, "Genre, Repetition and History in Jonathan Coe," *British Fiction Today,* ed. Philip Tew and Rod Mengham (London: Continuum, 2006), 31.
23. Hugh Barnes, "What a Carve Up!" *Scotsman,* May 28, 1994; Michiko Kakutani,

"Madcap Tale of a Family with Greed in Its Blood," *New York Times,* March 10, 1995, C30; Charles Gordon, "Satire on Nasty Thatcherite Elite Hits Targets with Bite and Wit," *Ottawa Citizen,* March 12, 1995, B4.

24. Florence Noiville, "The Contemporary British Novel—A French Perspective," *European Journal of English Studies* 10 (December 2006), 298.
25. Andrew Higson, "Fiction and the Film Industry," *A Concise Companion to Contemporary British Fiction,* ed. James F. English (Oxford: Blackwell, 2006), 61.
26. See Jonathan Coe, "My Favourite Hitchcock Film," *Observer,* June 16, 2012.
27. Frank King, *The Ghoul* (London: W. P. Nimmo, Hay and Mitchell, 1940), 5.
28. Simon Dentith, *Parody: The New Critical Idiom* (Abingdon, Oxon.: Routledge, 2000), 74.
29. Julia Llewellyn Smith, "Look Back in Anger and Satire," *Times,* February 23, 1995.
30. Terence Blacker, "Golden Slumbers: Night & Day," *Mail on Sunday,* May 25, 1997, 38.
31. Joel Yanofsky, "House of Sleep Is a Welcome Respite from Deep Thought: It's One Throwaway Gag after Another," *Gazette* (Montreal), March 28, 1998, 33.
32. Tom Lappin, "Sharp Satire Keeps One Awake in a World of Dreams," *Scotland on Sunday,* Mary 25, 1997, 13; J. Bottum, "Satirizing the Perpetual Sleepiness of the Modern World," *Washington Times,* March 15, 1998, B8; Erica Wagner, "Land of Nod and Wink," *Times,* May 24, 1997.
33. Coe, "Guardian Book Club: Week Three: Jonathan Coe on Writing What a Carve Up!" *Guardian*, April 16, 2011, Review, 6.
34. Baret Magarian, "What Happens if the Wrong Sort of Dreams Come True?" *Independent,* August 24, 1998, 13.
35. Peter O'Brien, "Sleeper Novel," *Globe and Mail,* March 28, 1998, D17.
36. Jonathan Coe, *The House of Sleep* (New York: Vintage Books, 1997),3.
37. Ben Platt, "A Mournful Mystery on England's Shore," NPR Books, January 29, 2009, http://www.npr.org/templates/story/story.php?storyId=100017442.
38. Suzanne Berne, "Snooze Alarm," *New York Times,* March 29, 1998.
39. Jonathan Coe, "*The House of Sleep,*" www.jonathancoewriter.com/books/houseOfSleep.html.
40. Charles Dickens, *Great Expectations* (New York: Walter J. Black, 1931), 598.
41. Michael Wood, "You See Stars," *London Review of Books,* June 19, 1997, 23.
42. David Nokes, "And So to Bed," *Sunday Times,* May 25, 1997.
43. Henna Venho, "'Nothing Lost Yet'—Loss as a Transforming Theme in Jonathan Coe's *The House of Sleep,*" M.A. thesis, University of Tampere, School of Modern Languages and Translation Studies, Autumn 2010: unpaginated.

FIVE: The Trotter Stories

1. Steven Zeitchik, "The Best Writer You've Never Heard Of," *Publisher's Weekly,* September 5, 2005, 22.
2. Tim Adams, "Likely Lads Return," *Guardian,* August 21, 2004, 14.
3. Christina Patterson, "The Way We Live Now," *Independent,* September 3, 2004, 20.
4. Jenny Turner, "The Pale People," *New York Times,* June 19, 2005.

5. Richard Eder, "When England Swung Like a Pendulum," *New York Times* March 24, 2002, Section 7, page 10.
6. Florence Noiville, "The Contemporary British Novel—A French Perspective," *European Journal of English Studies* 10 (December 2006), 298.
7. Chris Lehmann, "Dazed and Confused," *Washington Post Book World,* March 3, 2002, T07.
8. Simon Edge, "Jonathan Coe, the Man Who Satirised the 1980s, Goes Back to Schooldays," *Sunday Express,* February 18, 2001, 16.
9. William Sutcliffe, "Adolescent Britain," *Independent,* February 25, 2001, 40.
10. Quoted in Andrea Henry, "Trip Back to the '70s," *Mirror,* February 23, 2001, 23.
11. Pamela Thurschwell, "Genre, Repetition and History in Jonathan Coe," *British Fiction Today,* ed. Philip Tew and Rod Mengham (London: Continuum, 2006), 36.
12. John Mullan, *How Novels Work* (Oxford: Oxford University Press, 2006), 185.
13. Fyodor Dostoyevsky, *Crime and Punishment,* trans. Constance Garnett (New York: Modern Library, 1950), 532.
14. Jonathan Coe, *The Rotters' Club* (London: Viking, 2001), 403.
15. Lehmann, "Dazed and Confused," T07.
16. Francois Gallix and Vanessa Guignery, "Jonathan Coe," *Novelists in the New Millennium: Conversations with Writers,* ed. Vanessa Guignery (London: Palgrave Macmillan, 2013), 39.
17. Claus-Ulrich Viol, "Golden Years or Dark Ages? Cultural Memories of the 1970s in Recent British Fiction," *Twenty-First Century Fiction: Readings, Essays, Conversations, Anglistik und Englischunterricht,* ed. Christoph Ribbat (Heidelberg: Universitätsverlag Winter, 2005), 149–169.
18. David Renton, "The Killing of Blair Peach," *London Review of Books,* May 22, 2014, 23–26.
19. Stephen Amidon, "The Rotters' Club," *Atlantic Monthly,* May, 2002, 119.
20. Paul Gilroy, "The Closed Circle of Britain's Postcolonial Melancholia," *The Literature of Melancholia: Early Modern to Postmodern,* ed. Martin Middeke and Christina Wald (New York: Palgrave Macmillan, 2011), 200
21. Gallix and Guignery, "Jonathan Coe," 39.
22. Ian Sansom, "Through Plate-Glass," *London Review of Books,* May 10, 2001, 39; Adam Mars-Jones, "School's Out," *Observer,* February 25, 2001, 16.
23. Mullan, *How Novels Work,* 166; Mullan, "The Story Within," *Guardian,* February 26, 2005, 32.
24. "Author Enters Record Books with a 13,955-word Sentence," *Birmingham Post,* April 25, 2001, 3.
25. James Joyce, *Ulysses* (New York: Random House, 1961), 783.
26. "The Rotters' Club Gains 2.3m," *Broadcast,* January 27, 2005.
27. Carola Long, "Hot to Rot," *Times,* January 15, 2005, Features, 4.
28. David Cheal, "Return to the Forgotten Decade," *Daily Telegraph,* January 1, 2005, 10.
29. Jonathan Coe, *The Closed Circle* (London: Viking, 2004), 34.
30. Stephen Bernstein, "Jonathan Coe. *The Closed Circle,*" *Review of Contemporary Fiction,* September 22, 2006, 151.

31. Joy Press, "Fooled Brittania," *Village Voice,* May 17, 2005.
32. Jonathan Coe, "Moon Tunes," *Guardian,* July 11, 2008.
33. Elizabeth Judd, "After School," *Atlantic Monthly,* June 2005, 118.
34. Tom Lappin, "Noughties Boys," *Scotsman,* August 21, 2004, 12.
35. Steven Poole, "Squaring the Circle," *Guardian,* September 4, 2004, 23; Christopher Taylor, "Hindsight Tickling," *London Review of Books,* October 21, 2004, 12.
36. Ron Charles, "Rise of a Scoundrel," *Washington Post Book World,* June 5, 2005, T03.
37. Richard Mason, "The Dread Hand of Thatcher over Us All," *Independent on Sunday,* September 5, 2004, 35.

SIX: Later Novels

1. Toby Lichtig, "Pictures of You," *New Statesman,* September 20, 2007.
2. Frances Taliaferro, "The Photo Album," *Washington Post,* May 18, 2008, Book World 6.
3. Tom Lappin, "Family Saga Caught on Tape," *Scotsman,* September 1, 2007, 18
4. Quoted in John O'Connell, "Carving a New Path," *Time Out,* August 29, 2007, 48.
5. O'Connell, "Carving a New Path," 48.
6. Daniel Soar, "Beatrix and Rosamond," *London Review of Books,* October 18, 2007, 32.
7. Carmen Callil, "The Stories of Our Lives," *Guardian,* April 25, 2008, Review 4.
8. Quoted in Chris Lehmann, "The Counter-Family," *Nation,* May 26, 2008.
9. O'Connell, "Carving a New Path," 48.
10. Rosamond Lehmann, *The Ballad and the Source* (New York: Reynal and Hitchcock, 1945), 79.
11. Jonathan Coe, "My Literary Love Affair," *Guardian,* October 5, 2007, Review 4.
12. Jonathan Coe, introduction to Rosamond Lehmann, *Dusty Answer* (London: Flamingo, 1996), n.p.
13. Jan Bild, "Meet the Author: Jonathan Coe," The English Reading Group in Berlin, http://readinggroupberlin.wordpress.com/meet-the-author-jonathan-coe/.
14. Jonathan Coe, *The Rain Before It Falls* (New York: Alfred A. Knopf, 2008), 3.
15. Erica Wagner, "Caught on Tape," *New York Times,* April 13, 2008, BR8.
16. "The Rain Before It Falls," *Atlantic Monthly,* May 1, 2008.
17. Sophie Harrison, "Too Composed for Comfort," *Sunday Times,* September 9, 2007, 55.
18. Patrick Ness, "Only the Lonely," *Guardian,* September 8, 2007, 16.
19. Ian McGillis, "A Bitter Legacy," [Montreal] *Gazette,* March 22, 2008, 17.
20. David Robson, "Fiction: David Robson Is Impressed by the Male Foray into the Female Psyche," *Sunday Telegraph,* September 9, 2007, 46.
21. Bild, "Meet the Author: Jonathan Coe."
22. Philip Larkin, *The Complete Poems,* ed. Archie Burnett (New York: Farrar, Straus and Giroux, 2012), 88.
23. Lehmann, *The Ballad and the Source,* 79.
24. Adam Mars-Jones, "Secrets in a Cold Climate," *Observer,* September 15, 2007, Books 24.
25. Coe, "Literary Love Affair," Review 4.
26. Sam Leith, "The Loneliness of the Long-Distance Driver," *Prospect,* May 27, 2010.

27. William Giraldi, "The Man Who Fell in Love with His G.P.S.," *New York Times Sunday Book Review,* April 8, 2011, 8.
28. Jonathan Coe, "Jonathan Coe on Writing *What a Carve Up!*" *Guardian,* April 16, 2011, Review 6.
29. Jonathan Coe, *The Terrible Privacy of Maxwell Sim* (London: Viking, 2010), 87.
30. John Barber, "The 'Ordinary,'" *Globe and Mail,* March 22, 2011, R1.
31. Jonathan Derbyshire, "The Terrible Privacy of Maxwell Sim," *New Statesman,* May 31, 2010.
32. Jonathan Coe has used Mumsnet; on July 1, 2008, he took part in an online chat with Mumsnet users about *The Rain Before It Falls* (http://www.mumsnet.com/onlinechats/jonathan-coe).
33. Chris Barton, "Book Review: 'The Terrible Privacy of Maxwell Sim' by Jonathan Coe," *Los Angeles Times,* March 17, 2001; Alex Clark, "In for the Long Haul," *Guardian,* May 22, 2010, 6 ("Pooterish" refers to Mr. Pooter, the main character of the book *Diary of a Nobody,* written by George and Weedon Grossmith and published in 1892); Leith, "The Loneliness of the Long-Distance Driver."
34. Ed Park, "Only Disconnect," *Bookforum,* February/March 2011, http://www.bookforum.com/inprint/017_05/7018.
35. Leo Robson, "Out of Facebook, into Life," *Times,* May 15, 2010, 11.
36. Quoted in Kathleen Byrne, "Ordinary Man, Ordinary Madness," *Globe and Mail,* March 28, 2011, R4.
37. Virginia Woolf, *The Common Reader,* first and second series (New York: Harcourt, Brace and Company, 1925), 213.
38. Quoted in Paul Laity, "A Life in Writing: Jonathan Coe," *Guardian,* May 28, 2010, 12.
39. David Lodge, *The Modes of Modern Writing: Metaphor, Metonymy, and the Typology of Modern Literature* (Chicago: University of Chicago Press, 1977), 239.
40. Stefan Beck, "The Information," *New Criterion* (May 2011), 33.
41. Quoted in Barber, "The 'Ordinary,'" R1.
42. Quoted in Barber, "The 'Ordinary,'" R1.
43. Jonathan Coe, *Expo 58* (London: Viking, 2013), 18–19.
44. Peter Carty, "Back to the Future, Only in Belgium," *Independent,* September 8, 2013, 18.
45. Sarah A. Smith, "All's Fair in Love & War," *Literary Review,* September, 2013.
46. Clifford Armion, "An Interview with Jonathan Coe (Expo 58)," *Le Clé des Langues,* February 14, 2014. http://cle.ens-lyon.fr/anglais/an-interview-with-jonathan-coe-expo-58–222695.kjsp.
47. Alexis Liebaert, "Expo 58, un nid d'espions et de pieds nickelés," *Le Magazine Littéraire,* February 26, 2014.
48. Lucy Kellaway, "Review: 'Expo 58' by Jonathan Coe," *Financial Times,* August 30, 2013.
49. James Lasdun, "Expo 58 by Jonathan Coe—Review," *Guardian,* September 19, 2013, 11.
50. Jonathan Coe, *Expo 58* (http://www.jonathancoewriter.com/books/expo58.html).
51. Robert McCrum, "To Brussels via Ealing on HM's Service," *Observer,* September 7, 2013, Books 34.

52. Cressida Connolly, "Expo 58 by Jonathan Coe—Review," *Spectator,* September 21, 2013, 46.
53. Kate Kellaway, "The Save the Story Series by Various Authors—Review," *Observer,* November 17, 2013, Books 37.

Conclusion

1. Jonathan Coe, "Jonathan Coe on Writing What a Carve Up!" *Guardian,* April 16, 2011, Review 6.
2. Nick Rennison, *Contemporary British Novelists* (London: Routledge, 2005), 44.
3. William May," Closing the Circle: An Interview with Jonathan Coe," *From Self to Shelf: The Artist under Construction,* ed. Sally Bayley and William May (Newcastle: Cambridge Scholars, 2007), 71.
4. Jonathan Coe, *The House of Sleep* (New York: Vintage, 1997), 129
5. Flann O'Brien, *At Swim-Two-Birds* (New York: Plume, 1966), 33.
6. Nick Hornby, *Housekeeping vs. The Dirt* (San Francisco: Believer Books, 2006), 14.
7. Nick Hornby, *The Polysyllabic Spree* (San Francisco: Believer Books, 2004), 108.

BIBLIOGRAPHY

Works by Jonathan Coe

BOOKS

A Touch of Love. London: Penguin, 1989.

The Dwarves of Death. London: Penguin, 1990.

Humphrey Bogart: Take It and Like It. New York: Grove Weidenfeld, 1991.

Jimmy Stewart: A Wonderful Life. New York: Arcade Publishing, 1994.

What a Carve Up! London: Penguin, 1994.

The House of Sleep. New York: Vintage Books, 1997.

The Accidental Woman. 1987; London: Penguin, 2000.

The Rotters' Club. London: Viking, 2001.

Like a Fiery Elephant: The Story of B. S. Johnson. New York: Continuum, 2004.

The Closed Circle. London: Viking, 2004.

9th & 13th. London: Penguin, 2005.

The Rain Before It Falls. New York: Alfred A. Knopf, 2008.

The Terrible Privacy of Maxwell Sim. London: Viking, 2010.

Expo 58. London: Viking, 2013.

SHORTER WORKS

"Low Culture Rises above Its Critics." *Sunday Times*, November 20, 1994.

"Hammer's Cosy Violence." *Sight and Sound* 6 (August 1996): 10–11.

Introduction to Rosamond Lehmann, *Dusty Answer*. London: Flamingo, 1996, n.p.

Introduction to B. S. Johnson, *The Unfortunates*. London: Picador, 1999, v–xv.

Introduction to Rosamond Lehmann, *The Echoing Grove*. London: Virago, 2000, n.p.

"The Madness of King George: Power Mad." In *Film/Literature/Heritage: A Sight and Sound Reader*, ed. Ginette Vincenteau. London: British Film Institute, 2001, 135–138.

"Jonathan Coe." In *Mortification: Writers' Stories of Their Public Shame*, ed. Robin Robertson. New York: Fourth Estate, 2003, 148–149.

"'Great Spunky Unflincher': Laurence Sterne, B S Johnson and Me," *Shandean* 15 (2004): 9–29.

"My Literary Love Affair." *Guardian*, October 5, 2007, Review 4.

"Moon Tunes." *Guardian*, July 11, 2008.

"Author, Author: Aiming at a Beast Called 'Thatcherism.'" *Guardian*, April 10, 2009, 15.

"What's So Funny about the British?" *Times*, October 3, 2009, 42–43.

"Guardian Book Club: Week Three: Jonathan Coe on Writing What a Carve Up!" *Guardian*, April 16, 2011, Review, 6.
"My Favourite Hitchcock Film." *Guardian*, June 16, 2012.
Preface to B. S. Johnson, *Well Done God!*, ed. Jonathan Coe, Philip Tew, and Julia Jordan. London: Picador, 2013, xi-xiv.
"*Expo 58.*" *Jonathan Coe—Writer.* http://www.jonathancoewriter.com/books/expo58.html.
"*The House of Sleep.*" *Jonathan Coe—Writer.* http://www.jonathancoewriter.com/books/houseOfSleep.html.
"*The Terrible Privacy of Maxwell Sim.*" *Jonathan Coe—Writer.* http://www.jonathancoewriter.com/books/maxwellSim.html.
"Writing the Contemporary." *Jonathan Coe—Writer.* http://www.jonathancoewriter.com.

Secondary Sources

Adams, Tim. "Likely Lads Return." *Guardian*, August 21, 2004.
Akbar, Arifa. "Coe's 'Experimental' Biography Wins £30,000 Prize." *Independent*, June 15, 2005, 8.
Allen, Nicola. *Marginality in the Contemporary British Novel.* London: Continuum, 2008.
Amidon, Stephen. "The Rotters' Club." *Atlantic Monthly*, May 2002, 119–20.
Armion, Clifford. "An Interview with Jonathan Coe (Expo 58)." *Le Clé des Langues*, February 14, 2014. http://cle.ens-lyon.fr/anglais/an-interview-with-jonathan-coe-expo-58-222695.kjsp.
"Author Enters Record Books with a 13,955-word Sentence." *Birmingham Post*, April 25, 2001, 3.
Barber, John. "The 'Ordinary." *Globe and Mail*, March 22, 2011, R1.
Barnes, Hugh. "Carry on up the comic culture." *Independent*, April 24, 1994, 33.
Barnes, Hugh. "What a Carve Up!" *Scotsman*, May 28, 1994.
Barton, Chris. "Book Review: 'The Terrible Privacy of Maxwell Sim' by Jonathan Coe." *Los Angeles Times*, March 17, 2001.
Beck, Stefan. "The Information." *New Criterion*, May 2011, 32–37.
Berne, Suzanne. "Snooze Alarm." *New York Times*, March 29, 1998, Section 7, 2.
Bernstein, Stephen. "Jonathan Coe: *The Closed Circle.*" *Review of Contemporary Fiction*, September 22, 2006, 151.
Bild, Jan. "Meet the Author: Jonathan Coe." The English Reading Group in Berlin. http://readinggroupberlin.wordpress.com/meet-the-author-jonathan-coe/.
Blacker, Terence. "Golden Slumbers: Night & Day." *Mail on Sunday*, May 25, 1997, 38.
Bottum, J. "Satirizing the Perpetual Sleepiness of the Modern World." *Washington Times*, March 15, 1998, B8.
Bradford, Richard. *The Novel Now: Contemporary British Fiction.* Oxford: Blackwell, 2007.
Byrne, Kathleen. "Ordinary Man, Ordinary Madness." *Globe and Mail*, March 28, 2011, R4.
Callil, Carmen. "The Stories of Our Lives." *Guardian*, April 26, 2008, Review, 4.
Carty, Peter. "Back to the Future, Only in Belgium." *Independent*, September 8, 2013, 18.
Charles, Ron. "Rise of a Scoundrel." *Washington Post Book World*, June 5, 2005, T03.
Cheal, David. "Return to the Forgotten Decade." *Daily Telegraph*, January 1, 2005, 10.

Clark, Alex. "In for the Long Haul." *Guardian*, May 22, 2010, 6.

Connolly, Cressida. "Expo 58 by Jonathan Coe—Review." *Spectator*, September 21, 2013, 46.

Connolly, Cyril. *Enemies of Promise*. New York: Persea Books, 1983.

Cooke, Rachel. "The Man Who Hated Stories." *Observer*, May 29, 2004, 14.

Delingpole, James. "Laying It On a Bit Thick." *Spectator*, April 14, 2001, 34.

Delingpole, James. "Third Person Second Nature." *Daily Telegraph*, February 24, 2001, 7.

Dentith, Simon. *Parody: The New Critical Idiom*. Abingdon, Oxon.: Routledge, 2000.

Derbyshire, Jonathan. "The Terrible Privacy of Maxwell Sim." *New Statesman*, May 31, 2010.

Dickens, Charles. *Great Expectations*. New York: Walter J. Black, 1931.

Dostoyevsky, Fyodor. *Crime and Punishment*. Trans. Constance Garnett. New York: Modern Library, 1950.

Driscoll, Jonathan. *Evading Class in Contemporary British Literature*. London: Palgrave Macmillan, 2009.

Eagleton, Terry. "Theydunnit." *London Review of Books*, April 28, 1994, 12.

Eaton, Shirley. *Golden Girl*. London: B. T. Batsford, 1999.

Eder, Richard. "The House of Sleep." *Los Angeles Times*, March 1, 1998.

Eder, Richard. "When England Swung Like a Pendulum." *New York Times*, March 24, 2002, Section 7, page 10.

Edge, Simon. "Jonathan Coe, the Man Who Satirised the 1980s, Goes Back to Schooldays." *Sunday Express*, February 18, 2001, 16.

Evans, Julian. "Modernism's Suicide." *Prospect*, June 20, 2004.

Fielding, Henry. *The Adventures of Joseph Andrews*. London: Oxford University Press, 1961.

Gallix, François, and Vanessa Guignery. "Jonathan Coe." In *Novelists in the New Millennium: Conversations with Writers*, ed. Vanessa Guignery. London: Palgrave Macmillan, 2013, 27–43.

Gilroy, Paul. "The Closed Circle of Britain's Postcolonial Melancholia." In *The Literature of Melancholia: Early Modern to Postmodern*, ed. Martin Middeke and Christina Wald. New York: Palgrave Macmillan, 2011, 187–204.

Giraldi, Willam. "The Man Who Fell in Love with His G.P.S." *New York Times Sunday Book Review*, April 10, 2011, BR8.

Gordon, Charles. "Satire on Nasty Thatcherite Elite Hits Targets with Bite and Wit." *Ottawa Citizen*, March 12, 1995, B4.

Grimley, Terry. "A Bestseller Straight from 70s Brum." *Birmingham Post*, March 14, 2001, 13.

Guignery, Vanessa. *Jonathan Coe*. London: Palgrave Macmillan, 2016.

Hanks, Robert. "Modern Life's a Rotten Disappointment." *Independent*, October 8, 2004, 35.

Harrison, Sophie. "Too Composed for Comfort." *Sunday Times*, September 9, 2007, 55.

Head, Dominic. "The Demise of Class Fiction." In *A Concise Companion to Contemporary British Fiction*, ed. James F. English. Oxford: Blackwell, 2006, 229–47.

Head, Dominic. *The Cambridge Introduction to Modern British Fiction, 1950–2000*. Cambridge: Cambridge University Press, 2002.

Henry, Andrea. "Trip Back to the '70s." *The Mirror,* February 23, 2001, 23.

Higson, Andrew. "Fiction and the Film Industry." In *A Concise Companion to Contemporary British Fiction,* ed. James F. English. Oxford: Blackwell, 2006, 58–79.

Hornby, Nick. *Housekeeping vs. the Dirt.* San Francisco: Believer Books, 2006.

Hornby, Nick. *The Polysyllabic Spree.* San Francisco: Believer Books, 2004.

Johnson, B. S. *Christie Malry's Own Double-Entry.* New York: New Directions, 2009.

Joyce, James. *Ulysses.* New York: Random House, 1961.

Judd, Elizabeth. "After School." *Atlantic Monthly,* June 2005, 118.

Kakutani, Michiko. "Madcap Tale of a Family with Greed in Its Blood." *New York Times,* March 10, 1995, C30.

Kellaway, Kate. "The Save the Story Series by Various Authors—Review." *Observer,* November 17, 2013, Books, 37.

Kellaway, Lucy. "Review: 'Expo 58' by Jonathan Coe." *Financial Times,* August 30, 2013.

Kermode, Frank. "Retripotent." *London Review of Books,* August 5, 2004, 11–13.

King, Frank. *The Ghoul.* London: W. P. Nimmo, Hay and Mitchell, 1940.

Koning, Christina. "Anything but the Girl." *Guardian,* May 17, 1990.

Laity, Paul. "A Life in Writing: Jonathan Coe." *Guardian,* May 28, 2010, 12.

Lanchester, John. "Strong Meat." *London Review of Books,* January 11, 1990, 11.

Lappin, Tom. "Family Saga Caught on Tape." *Scotsman,* September 1, 2007, 18.

Lappin, Tom. "Noughties Boys." *Scotsman,* August 21, 2004, 12.

Lappin, Tom. "Sharp Satire Keeps One Awake in a World of Dreams." *Scotland on Sunday,* May 25, 1997, 13

Lappin, Tom. "Waiting for Tony." *Scotland on Sunday,* August 17, 1997, Spectrum 11.

Larkin, Philip. *The Complete Poems,* ed. Archie Burnett. New York: Farrar, Straus and Giroux, 2012.

Lasdun, James. "Expo 58 by Jonathan Coe—Review." *Guardian,* September 21, 2013, 11.

Le Dour-Zana, Corinne. "Jonathan Coe fait ses gammes," *Plume Noir.* www.plume-noir.com/culture/livres/lesnainsetlamort.html.

Lehmann, Chris. "Dazed and Confused." *Washington Post Book World,* March 3, 2002, T07.

Lehmann, Chris. "The Counter-Family." *Nation,* May 26, 2008.

Lehmann, Rosamond. *The Ballad and the Source.* New York: Reynal and Hitchcock, 1945.

Leith, Sam. "The Loneliness of the Long-Distance Driver." *Prospect,* May 27, 2010.

Lichtig, Toby. "Pictures of You." *New Statesman,* September 20, 2007.

Liebaert, Alexis. "Expo 58, un nid d'espions et de pieds nickelés," *Le Magazine Littéraire,* February 26, 2014.

Llewellyn Smith, Julia. "Look Back in Anger and Satire." *Times,* February 23, 1995.

Lodge, David. *The Modes of Modern Writing: Metaphor, Metonymy, and the Typology of Modern Literature.* Chicago: University of Chicago Press, 1977.

Long, Carola. "Hot to Rot." *Times,* January 15, 2005, Features, 4.

Magarian, Baret."What Happens if the Wrong Sort of Dreams Come True?" *Independent,* August 24, 1998, 13.

Mars-Jones, Adam. "School's Out." *Observer,* February 25, 2001, 16.

Mars-Jones, Adam. "Secrets in a Cold Climate." *Observer,* September 6, 2007, Books, 24.

Mason, Richard. "The Dread Hand of Thatcher over Us All." *Independent on Sunday,* September 5, 2004, 35.

May, William. "Closing the Circle: An Interview with Jonathan Coe." In *From Self to Shelf: The Artist under Construction,* ed. Sally Bayley and William May. Newcastle: Cambridge Scholars Publishing, 2007, 66–75.

McCrum, Robert. "To Brussels via Ealing on HM's Service." *Observer,* September 8, 2013, Books, 34.

McGillis, Ian. "A Bitter Legacy." *Gazette* (Montreal), March 22, 2008, 17.

Mullan, John. *How Novels Work.* Oxford: Oxford University Press, 2006.

Mullan, John. "The Story Within." *Guardian* February 26, 2005, 32.

Ness, Patrick. "Only the Lonely." *Guardian,* September 8, 2007, 16.

Noiville, Florence. "The Contemporary British Novel—A French Perspective." *European Journal of English Studies* 10 (December 2006): 297–300.

Nokes, David. "And So To Bed." *Sunday Times,* May 25, 1997.

O'Brien, Flann. *At Swim-Two-Birds.* New York: Plume, 1966.

O'Brien, Peter. "Sleeper Novel." *Globe and Mail,* March 28, 1998, D17.

O'Connell, John. "Carving a New Path." *Time Out,* August 29, 2007, 48.

Park, Ed. "Only Disconnect." *Bookforum,* February/March 2011. http://www.bookforum.com/inprint/017_05/7018.

Patterson, Christina. "The Way We Live Now." *Independent,* September 3, 2004, 20.

Platt, Ben. "A Mournful Mystery on England's Shore." NPR books, January 29, 2009. http://www.npr.org/templates/story/story.php?storyId=100017442.

Poole, Steven. "Squaring the Circle." *Guardian,* September 4, 2004, 23.

Portesi, Bruno. "Confusion des sentiments," Parutions.com, March 3, 2004. http://www.parutions.com/?pid=1&rid=15&srid=162&ida=4147.

Potter, Jennifer. "Paisley Pattern Plot: 'The Dwarves of Death.'" *Independent,* May 27, 1990, 19.

Press, Joy. "Fooled Brittania." *Village Voice,* May 17, 2005.

Quinn, Anthony. "Clawing, Brutish Gargoyles." *Independent,* April 23, 1994, 26.

"The Rain Before It Falls." *Atlantic Monthly,* May 1, 2008.

Rennison, Nick. *Contemporary British Novelists.* London: Routledge, 2005.

Renton, David. "The Killing of Blair Peach." *London Review of Books,* May 22, 2014, 23–26.

Robson, David. "Fiction: David Robson Is Impressed by the Male Foray into the Female Psyche." *Sunday Telegraph,* September 9, 2007, 46.

Robson, Leo. "Out of Facebook, into Life." *Times,* May 15, 2010, 11.

"The Rotters' Club Gains 2.3m." *Broadcast,* January 27, 2005, www.broadcastnow.co.uk.

Sanderson, Mark. "Mark Sanderson Finds an Unexceptional Man's Sad Life Both Compelling and Funny." *Daily Telegraph,* May 30, 2010, 30.

Sansom, Ian. "Through Plate-Glass" *London Review of Books,* May 10, 2001, 39.

Smith, Sarah A. "All's Fair in Love & War." *Literary Review,* September 2013.

Soar, Daniel. "Beatrix and Rosamond." *London Review of Books* October 18, 2007, 32–33.

Sutcliffe, William. "Adolescent Britain." *Independent,* February 25, 2001, 40.

Sutton, Henry. "Life beyond Hampstead: Gritty, Politically Engaged Novels Are Rare These Days." *Independent on Sunday* November 2, 2003, 16.

Symons, Julian. "Deep Down." *London Review of Books,* June 28, 1990, 20–21.

Taliaferro, Frances. "The Photo Album." *Washington Post,* May 18, 2008, Book World, 6.

Taylor, Christopher. "Hindsight Tickling." *London Review of Books,* October 21, 2004, 12.

Tew, Philip, "Jonathan Coe." In *Writers Talk: Conversations with Contemporary British Novelists,* edited by Philip Tew, Fiona Tolan, and Leigh Wilson, 35–56. London: Continuum, 2008.

Thurschwell, Pamela. "Genre, Repetition and History in Jonathan Coe." In *British Fiction Today,* ed. Philip Tew and Rod Mengham. London: Continuum, 2006, 28–39.

Thwaite, Anthony. "A Novelist, but Not So Novel." *Sunday Telegraph,* June 6, 2004, 13.

Trimm, Ryan. "Carving Up Value: The Tragicomic Thatcher Years in Jonathan Coe." In *Thatcher & After: Margaret Thatcher and Her Afterlife in Contemporary Culture,* ed. Louisa Hadley and Elizabeth Ho. Basingston. Hants: Palgrave Macmillan, 2010, 158–79.

Turner, Jenny. "The Pale People." *New York Times,* June 19, 2005.

Venho, Henna. "'Nothing Lost Yet'—Loss as a Transforming Theme in Jonathan Coe's *The House of Sleep.*" M.A. thesis, University of Tampere, School of Modern Languages and Translation Studies, 2010.

Vianu, Lidia. "The Accidental Theme: Jonathan Coe, The Accidental Woman." *Philologica Jassyensia,* 4 (2008): 147–65.

Vincent, Sally. "A Bit of a Rotter" *Guardian Weekend,* February 23, 2001, 36.

Viol, Claus-Ulrich. "Golden Years or Dark Ages? Cultural Memories of the 1970s in Recent British Fiction." In *Twenty-first Century Fiction: Readings, Essays, Conversations, Anglistik und Englischunterricht,* ed. Christoph Ribbat. Heidelberg: Universitätsverlag Winter, 2005, 149–169.

Wagner, Erica. "Caught on Tape." *New York Times,* April 13, 2008, BR8.

Wagner, Erica. "Land of Nod and Wink." *Times,* May 24, 1997.

Waugh, Patricia. *Metafiction: The Theory and Practice of Self-Conscious Fiction.* London: Methuen, 1984.

Winder Robert. "A One-Man Avant-Garde." *New Statesman,* June 21, 2004.

Wood, Michael. "You See Stars." *London Review of Books,* June 19, 1997, 23.

Woolf, Virginia. *The Common Reader.* First and Second Series. New York: Harcourt, Brace and Company, 1925.

Yanofsky, Joel. "Comic Novel Has Message about '80s." *Gazette* (Montreal), March 18, 1995, H2.

Yanofsky, Joel. "House of Sleep Is a Welcome Respite from Deep Thought: It's One Throwaway Gag after Another." *Gazette* (Montreal), March 28, 1998, 33.

Zeitchik, Steven. "The Best Writer You've Never Heard Of." *Publisher's Weekly,* September 5, 2005, 21–22.

INDEX